DESIGN

The 50 most influential designers in the world

First published in Great Britain in 2009

A & C Black Publishers Ltd

London W1D 3QY

www.acblack.com

Copyright © Elwin Street Limited 2009

ISBN: 978 1 408 10630 3

Conceived and produced by
Elwin Street Limited
144 Liverpool Road
London N1 1LA
United Kingdom
www.elwinstreet.com

Jacket Design: Diana Sullada
Picture credits: Alamy: p. 5, 8, 19, 35, 38, 41, 42, 47, 52, 54, 63, 73, 76, 79, 85, 87, 93, 95, 99, 103, 105, 123, 126; The Art Archive: p. 56 (Private Collection/Alfredo Dagli Orti): p. 21, 31, 89, (Galerie J. J. Dutko Paris / Gianni Dagli Orti): p. 51, (Nicolas Sapieha): p. 117; Corbis: p. 15, 26, 28, 49, 65, 67, 71, DK Images: p. 36; Dreamstime: p. 5, 11, 24, 109, 112, 115, 119, 121; Getty: p. 4, 61; iStockphoto: p. 4, 7, 17, 69, 83; Photo Library: p. 80; Rex: p. 97, 107. Jacket picture credits: Alamy

A CIP catalogue record for this book is available from the British Library.

Printed in Singapore

DESIGN

The 50 most influential designers in the world

PAUL RODGERS

CONTENTS

Home Wares

Automotive

INTRODUCTION

Ultimately, design is concerned with enriching people's lives. Good design is the development of products, services and systems that can make positive changes to people's lives. This added value may be in the form of a more functionally robust product, a less expensive service or a system that reduces damage to the environment.

This book features designers who are responsible for many of the most significant developments in automotive and product design as well as in engineering, interiors, furniture, textiles, architecture and lighting. All the designers contained here have been able to exploit the technological, social and cultural developments of their time and transform them into momentous objects, systems and services that have enhanced our lives. Without these individuals and their developments – the car assembly and mass-production lines of Henry Ford, the democratic design philosophy of William Morris and the experimental and explorative design work of Charles and Ray Eames – the world as we know it today would be a far less wonderful place.

Yet the actual meaning of the word 'design' can be confusing, and is often subject to debate. The dictionary tells us that design, as a verb, is an activity that involves planning and marking out with the purpose and intention of creating something, such as clothes or products. As a noun, it means a plan conceived in the mind, of something to be done, such as a set of drawings showing how a building or product is to be made and how it will work and look. Typically, however, 'design' is used to refer to a process (the act of designing), that leads either to a sketch, plan or model, or eventually to an end product.

Creativity generates ideas and innovation exploits them – and design connects the two. The process of design involves many specialists including designers, engineers and marketing individuals all pulling together to create functional and appealing goods for consumers. It helps to create wealth and generate value, and its value can be measured economically, socially and environmentally.

We live in an almost completely designed world. We are surrounded by a multitude of designed products, spaces, systems, services and experiences that have been created in recognition of some physical, emotional, social, cultural or economic need. But design involves more than just the creation of things. It also includes the generation of ideas, the development of concepts, product testing and manufacturing and the implementation of a physical object, system or service. Designers conceptualise and evaluate ideas, making them tangible through products in a systematic manner, which encompasses characteristics of other disciplines including marketing, management and engineering. The role of a designer combines art, science, economics and commerce in one united form.

The 50 designers in this book have been selected for the contributions they have made to the designed world between the mid eighteenth century and the present day. They include technological innovators, such as James Dyson; pioneers of classic furniture and incredible domestic products, from Alvar Aalto to Philippe Starck; and radical automotive designers such as Alec Issigonis and Ferdinand Porsche.

Any selection is subjective and, undeniably, many convincing arguments could be made for the inclusion of other individuals. However, what is certain is the massive mark that each of these 50 designers has made in their own unique way.

The First Industrial Designer
Peter Behrens

Peter Behrens is viewed as one of the pioneers of modern, objective, industrial architecture and design. Responsible for bringing forth some of the most outstanding works in painting, architecture, graphic and industrial design during the twentieth century, his contributions in these various creative fields opened up unchartered territory for generations to come.

Born 1868, Hamburg, Germany
Importance Early pioneer of corporate identity
Died 1940, Berlin, Germany

Behrens studied at the Hamburg School of Art before attending art school in Karlsruhe and the Düsseldorfer Akademie from 1886 to 1889. He was initially employed as a painter and illustrator, and collaborated on designing the Berlin journal *Pan*, in 1898.

At the turn of the twentieth century, along with Bruno Paul, Richard Riemerschmid, Hermann Obrist, August Endell and Bernhard Pankok, Behrens co-founded the Vereinigte Werkstätten für Kunst im Handwerk (United Workshops) in Munich, producing handmade utilitarian objects. He was also an important member of the Mathildenhöhe artists' colony, established by Grand Duke Ernst

Ludwig II von Hesse in Darmstadt. It was in Darmstadt that Behrens designed his first building – the Behrens House – conceived as a *Gesamtkunstwerk* (complete art work) because Behrens designed all the furniture and glassware specifically for it. This house marked an important transition point in Behrens' career, where he departed away from Jugendstil (the German term for the Art Nouveau movement) meotowards a more rational design approach.

Today, Behrens is probably best known for his crisp, modern metalwork designs for AEG (Allgemeine Elektrizitäts Gesellschaft) – eminently practical, yet handsome, examples of mass production made to an exceptionally high standard. AEG had hired Behrens in 1907 as an independent artistic adviser, after which he was responsible for the company's entire corporate identity. He designed the AEG Turbine Factory in 1908 – one of the first true expressions of modern industrial architecture. He also undertook the design of electrical products such as kettles, clocks and fans, incorporating standardised components that were interchangeable between products so as to rationalise production. He also had overall responsibility for the graphics and corporate identity of AEG. This was the first time a company had employed a designer to advise on all aspects of design and, because of his ability to work across design disciplines in this way, he is considered the first industrial designer in history.

From 1907 to 1912, Behrens had students and assistants, among whom were some of the biggest names in the history of design such as Ludwig Mies van der Rohe, Le Corbusier and Walter Gropius. Today, Peter Behrens' simple, practical and rational design solutions are viewed as hugely important in the formation and dissemination of modernism, while his pioneering corporate identity work for AEG has been seen to have a massive influence on later companies' house-design strategies, such as Braun.

Walter Dorwin Teague

Referred to by many as the 'dean of industrial design', Walter Dorwin Teague was the founder-director of what was arguably America's first industrial design company. One of an elite group of designers, Teague helped shape the concept of the 'consultant' industrial designer. He was a major player in developing the distinctive streamlining style that has come to represent what is now known as the 'machine age'.

Born 1883, Pendleton, Indiana, United States
Importance Founded the industrial design industry in America
Died 1960, Flemington, New Jersey, United States

Teague studied painting at the Art Students League, in New York, between 1903 and 1907, and began his professional career as a graphic designer, illustrating magazines and mail-order catalogues. He then worked as an advertising illustrator, in particular for Calkins and Holden. He established his own graphic design and typographic studio in 1912 and, by the mid 1920s, was involved in commercial packaging.

In 1926, while travelling in Europe, he discovered the work of Le Corbusier and, on returning to New York, he founded Walter Dorwin Teague Associates in order to pursue a career in designing, or restyling, products for manufacturers. At the time he was one of a handful of individuals in New York – including Norman Bel Geddes, Raymond Loewy and Henry Dreyfuss – who were starting to establish industrial design as an independent occupation, promoted by the foundation of the American Union of Decorative Artists and Craftsmen.

Teague received his first contract, with Eastman Kodak, early in 1928. His first camera, the Vanity Kodak (1928), was designed specifically for the female market and was produced in a series of different colours with matching silk-lined cases. He designed the classic Baby Brownie camera (1933) – one of the first consumer products made of plastic – the compact and user-friendly Bantam

Special (1936), the Kodak Super 620 (1938) and the Brownie Hawkeye (1950). Teague was also responsible for the first Polaroid camera for Edwin Land. Teague and the Baby Brownie camera have since become synonymous names in the history of twentieth-century design.

In 1930, Teague designed the Marmon *Model 16* car, one of the most aerodynamically efficient cars of its time. He was also responsible for the trendsetting Texaco petrol stations of the mid 1930s, as well as many other streamlined products for his long list of blue-chip clients. The streamlined style he pioneered reached its pinnacle at the World's Fair of 1939 in New York, for which Teague designed the Ford and US Steel pavilions.

Teague's best-selling book, *Design This Day – The Technique of Order in the Machine Age* (1940), celebrated the potential of machines and the 'new and thrilling style' of the modern era. He is widely considered one of the founding fathers of American design and, in 1944, became the first president of the American Society of Industrial Designers. After the Second World War, Walter Dorwin Teague Associates became a major consultant for Boeing, establishing a branch office in Seattle, and has designed interiors for them ever since. After Teague's death in 1960, his son, Walter Dorwin Teague Jr, continued to run the firm from their headquarters in Redmond, Washington.

STREAMLINING

Streamlining was a concept that burst on to the design scene in 1930s America. Primarily it was seen as a backlash to the prevailing art deco and modernist movements that were demanding the attention of leading designers across the Atlantic in western Europe.

This new design movement was applied to a vast array of products, from buses to coffee machines to pencil sharpeners, and was widely employed by American architects and designers from around the early 1930s onwards. In many respects, it became the defining style of the period. Although considered by many to be an American development, streamlining was in fact an invention of the Italian futurist movement that began in the early twentieth century.

Streamlining is literally the shaping of an object, such as an aircraft body or wing, to reduce the amount of drag, or resistance to motion, through a stream of air – in essence producing an aerodynamic form. This idealised water-drop form minimises wind resistance and allows air to flow smoothly around it. Streamlining has been used in the styling of various products to symbolise a dynamic faith in the future and, since the 1950s, has been used by most of the industrialised nations of the world.

After the Wall Street Crash of 1929, and the resulting Great Depression, together with the implementation of the price-fixing National Recovery Act of 1932, many manufacturers in the United States were forced to restyle or 'streamline' their products in a bid to stay in business. This involved redesigning their existing wares in order to make them appear brand new, instead of investing time and money in the development of entirely new products. It was around this time that the term 'styling' first appeared in design circles and was used to describe this formal reworking of a product under purely aesthetic and market-oriented considerations so that it became more attractive to the consumer and thus gave the American economy a much-needed boost.

The concept of streamlining was applied to many items during the Great Depression years, and was often used as an antidote to the predominantly grey mood of the country. The glamour and futuristic aesthetic of streamlining could now be seen in a wide range of products, and was particularly heavily used in transport design such as automobiles, trains and airships. Based on the visual rules of aerodynamic efficiency, wherein forms would be designed to minimise resistance to wind or water, the concept was used in so many products in America during the 1930s that the entire period has been described by commentators as 'the streamlined decade'.

'Streamlining has taken the world by storm.'

Industrial designer, Harold van Doren

The practice of streamlining helped many manufacturers differentiate their products from those of their competitors and some companies even used annual restyling programmes to accelerate the aesthetic obsolescence of products in an effort to increase sales. Streamlining was used by many designers to evoke an image of a glowing future, and the key figures in the era of streamlining and styling of products were Raymond Loewy, Norman Bel Geddes, Henry Dreyfuss and Walter Dorwin Teague, who rapidly became household names.

Raymond Loewy

From the 1930s until his retirement in the 1970s, Americans could barely take a step without encountering Loewy's creative touch in their homes, in their offices and in their airports, train stations and motorway networks. A leader in popularising the look that came to dominate design in mid twentieth century America, Loewy replaced the dark, heavy aesthetic of the previous generation with a streamlined look dominated by curves based on the aerodynamic shapes of planes and ships.

Born 1893, Paris, France
Importance One of the world's first 'consultant' designers
Died 1986, Monte Carlo, Monaco

Dedicated to the field of industrial design, Loewy worked as a consultant for more than 200 companies, creating designs for almost everything – from cigarette packets and fridges, to cars, trains and spacecraft.

His first design commission was for Gestetner, a British manufacturer of duplicating machines, in 1929. He was commissioned to improve the appearance of the Gestetner Ream Duplicator 66 machine and, within three days, he had designed the shell that was to encase Gestetner duplicators for the next 40 years. Many believe that Loewy's success owes much to his understanding that industrial design was basically about advertising and selling and not about truth to materials and honest functions. His reputation as a fierce self-promoter was evident in the fact that he had cards printed with the phrase – 'Between two products equal in price, function and quality, the better looking will outsell the other'.

Loewy spent more than five decades streamlining and

'I can claim to have made the daily life of the twentieth century more beautiful.'

modernising silverware and fountain pens, supermarkets and department stores. He and his team also designed the colour scheme and logos for Lucky Strike cigarettes, Air Force One, the John F Kennedy memorial stamp, Pennsylvania Railroad locomotives and advertising materials, and the interiors for NASA's Skylab. His prestigious clientele included such icons as Coca-Cola, Exxon, Nabisco, Canada Dry, Pepsodent, British Petroleum, Electrolux, Coldspot and Greyhound Buses.

In 1949, Loewy became the first designer to be featured on the front cover of *Time* magazine, his picture accompanied by the unforgettable caption: 'He streamlines the sales curve'. He had the eye of an artist but he also had the mind of a businessman. In his hands industrial design became an important marketing tool. He knew that the consumer did not live by logic alone and understood that advertising, packaging and product design was the holy trinity of consumer seduction. Though never shy about the commercial intent of his products, Loewy saw himself more as a white knight of design.

INDUSTRIAL DESIGN
The general term used to describe the design and development of any mass-produced product.

Henry Dreyfuss

A prolific and highly successful designer of the interwar period, Henry Dreyfuss' greatest contribution to industrial design was his research into anthropometrics. He is credited with pioneering the application of ergonomic principles (see page 22) in industrial design.

Born 1904, New York, United States
Importance
Groundbreaking American industrial designer of products from telephones to trains
Died 1972, South Pasadena, California, United States

Henry Dreyfuss was born to a family in the theatrical materials supply business. He trained at the Ethical Culture School in New York prior to completing his studies as an apprentice to the industrial designer Norman Bel Geddes. He opened his own design office, in 1929, for stage and industrial design activities.

One of Dreyfuss' earliest designed products was his Bell Model 300 telephone (1937). The company approached Dreyfuss when he won a 'Telephone of the Future' competition in 1929. His design had been the first ever to incorporate both the mouthpiece and the receiver in a single component. This was the start of a healthy collaborative partnership that would last for several decades. He also designed other telephones for Bell including the Model 500 (1949) and the Trimline (1964). In 1949, the Model 500 telephone was put into service by AT&T. The first to be offered in colours other than black (from 1954), the Model 500 was still the most commonly used telephone in the US four decades later, in 1995.

Dreyfuss' straightforward approach to the design process contributed significantly to the success of his design office. His large corporate clientele resulted in his office producing a variety of work such as a new 'flat-top' deluxe refrigerator for General Electric (1933), a washing machine for Sears & Roebuck, alarm clocks for Westclox (including their famous Big Ben alarm clock in 1939), Hoover's

Model 150 upright vacuum cleaner with the first plastic hood in
Bakelite (1936) and a flask for The American Thermos Bottle
Company (1936).

Between 1938 and 1940, Dreyfuss designed two trains for the
New York Central Railroad. He also designed military equipment,
farm machinery, televisions, the Polaroid Model 100 camera and the
General Motors Futurama Exhibition for the 1964 World's Fair in
New York. In 1944, Dreyfuss was a founder member of the Society of
Industrial Designers (SID) and served as its first vice president. He was
also the first president of the Industrial Designers Society of America
(IDSA) and appeared on the front cover of *Forbes Magazine* in 1951.

In 1955, Dreyfuss published the first of his two books, *Designing
for People,* which included the first publication of scale drawings and
anthropological charts of 'Mr and Mrs Average'. In 1960, The
Whitney Library of Design published his second book, *The Measure of
Man: Human Factors in Design.* An ergonomic data guide compiled
from military records, the book also featured Mr and Mrs
Average, and popularised the idea of fitting products
to human scale (see page 22). Dreyfuss focused
on design problems relating to the human
figure, working on problems from
'the inside out', and believed that
machines adapted to people
would be the most efficient.

Marcello Nizzoli

Heavily influenced by the organic aesthetic, Marcello Nizzoli's range of creative work extended to producing a range of sculptural designs, such as sewing machines for Mirella and Necchi, kitchen equipment for Necchi and furniture for Arflex. He is best known for the range of work that he conducted for the office equipment company, Olivetti.

Born 1887, Boretto, Italy
Importance Among the first designers to beautify ordinary objects
Died 1969, Carnogli, Italy

Nizzoli studied art, architecture and graphic design at the School of Fine Art, Parma, from 1910 to 1913, after which he worked as an artist and industrial designer. He exhibited with the futurist group Nuove Tendenze (New Tendencies) in Milan in 1914. His design career took off in Milan, in 1918, where he established his own design studio and worked for over 20 years in exhibition, fabric and graphic design. Between 1934 and 1936, he worked in collaboration with the architect, Edoardo Persico, designing two Parker Pen shops and the Hall of Gold Medals for the 1934 'Aeronautical Exhibition' in Milan.

Adriano Olivetti (1901–60), son of founder Camillo, instigated the company's programme of employing consultant designers and Nizzoli began working there in 1938, initially as a graphic designer in the advertising department. Nizzoli's interest in organic forms was inspired by the likes of Henry Moore and Gio and Arnaldo Pomodoro, and is obvious in

Olivetti's products… seem almost illuminated by their exact proportions and the love with which an object should be constructed'

Le Corbusier on Nizzoli's work for Olivetti

much of his work for Olivetti. His first product for the company was an adding machine, the Divisumma 14 (1947), but his designs for typewriters have attracted most attention. The Lexicon 80 manual typewriter (1948), the Suma adding machine (1949) and the Lettera 22 portable typewriter (1950) are three of the most significant examples of his work for Olivetti. The Lettera 22 is heralded as his finest work for the company in the way it achieves architectural balance and sculptural form in an attractive integration of protective metal housing and internal mechanical components. The sleek fluid lines of the machine, and its low profile – offered in a variety of colours – made a dramatic break from the rest of the competing cumbersome and dull designs of office equipment of the time.

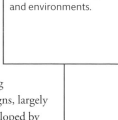

AESTHETIC
The word aesthetic, within the context of design, relates to the visual characteristics of products, buildings and environments.

Nizzoli paid loving attention to all details in his industrial design work, including the precise placement of controls and buttons and the location of surface components. He carefully integrated innovative engineering components and machinery beneath his fluid, organic designs, largely made possible by die-casting techniques that had been developed by Italy's booming steel industry of the period.

Nizzoli was distinguished with the Compasso d'Oro (see page 31) prize in 1954 for the Lettera 22 portable typewriter and, in 1959, the Illinois Institute of Technology selected the Lettera 22 as the best design product of the last 100 years.

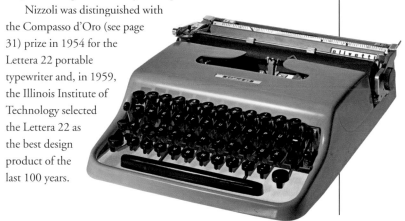

Marco Zanuso

Marco Zanuso is one of the founding fathers of Italian design, shaping both architecture and industrial design since 1945, and just one of a handful of designers contributing to the post-Second World War debate on the 'modern movement'. A leading light, Zanuso was one of the very first designers to become interested in the problems of mass-producing a product and applying new materials and technologies to everyday objects.

Born 1916, Milan, Italy
Importance Pioneered new materials and production processes
Died 2001, Milan, Italy

Zanuso studied architecture at Milan Polytechnic, graduating in 1939. He was editor in chief at *Domus* design magazine from 1947 to 1949 and, from 1952 to 1954, he edited the design magazine *Casabella*. In 1956, he co-founded the Associazione di Disegno Industriale (ADI) and acted as its president from 1966 to 1969.

Among his most important architectural works are the Olivetti industrial plants in São Paolo (1955) and Buenos Aires (1955–1957), and the Necchi factory in Pavia (1961–1962). He has been awarded many international prizes at various Milan Triennials and has received several Compasso d'Oro (see page 31) design awards, including one

'There is no dividing line between craft and design. Coming up with a prototype involves all our craft, industrial and academic experience. The fact that 50,000 copies of the finished object are then produced by a machine is a coincidence that goes under the name of industrial design.'

for his Model 1100/2 sewing machine for Borlett in 1956 and another in 1979 for the Ariante fan he created for Vortice.

Zanuso is a significant figure in post-war Italian design because of his experimentation and exploitation of new materials and production processes, as well as his rational, yet sculptural, approach to industrial design. His Antropus chair (1949) was created in response to a new material – latex foam – developed by Pirelli, the Italian tyre company. This was followed by several other latex-foam upholstered-chair designs such as the Lady chair (1951) and the Triennale sofa (1951), which were first exhibited at the IX Milan Triennial, where he won a Grand Prix and two gold medals. The Lambda chair (1962) was the result of another experiment – this time with enamelled sheet metal.

MILAN TRIENNIAL
A major design institution since 1923, the Milan Triennial is an annual exhibition of leading contemporary design work in architecture, furniture and interior design.

Through the 1950s and 1960s, Zanuso's long and prestigious working relationship with Richard Sapper resulted in many landmark product and furniture designs including children's stacking chairs (1964), which saw the first-ever application of polyethylene in a piece of furniture, and the moulded-plastic Grillo telephone for Siemens, with an in-built dial. With these products, and many others, Zanuso demonstrated the aesthetic potential of modern materials and mass-production technologies in the hands of a designer who understood not only how they worked, but also what they stood for in contemporary society.

ERGONOMICS

The relatively new science of ergonomics (known in the United States as Human Factors Engineering), involves the design of products, spaces and systems in such a way that end-users can employ them easily and comfortably, while gaining maximum efficiency at the same time. In the broadest terms, it is about ensuring a good fit between human beings and the products, equipment and facilities with which they interact on a daily basis as they work, travel, rest and play.

The word 'ergonomics' derives from two Greek words: *ergon*, meaning 'work', and *nomos*, meaning 'laws'. The contemporary use of the word is employed widely to describe the science of designing an object or environment to fit a person, and applies to a wide range of domestic scenarios in which humans rely on products to perform a desired action.

However, the term also extends to other, more important, contexts within work settings and the associated implications for efficiency, productivity and health and safety. For example, ergonomics can be used in designing products and systems, including machinery, so that they are easier to use and less likely to lead to errors in operation; equipment that improves working posture and eases the load on the body, thus reducing problems such as repetitive strain injury (RSI); and working environments that suit the needs of the users. Ergonomics can also be applied to the design of information that makes the interpretation and use of guidebooks, symbols and visual displays easier and less prone to errors.

Anthropometry is a branch of ergonomics that includes the study and recording of the physical shape and size of the human body including volumes, centres of gravity, inertial properties and masses of body segments. The name derives from *anthropos*, meaning 'human', and *metrikos*, meaning 'of, or pertaining to, measuring' – in other words, human measurement. Anthropometric measurements are generally taken of a particular cross-section of people, and are usually categorised along gender and age-range differences. Typical anthropometric data includes height, weight, arm reach, finger lengths and stride lengths, but also other measurements, such as lifting strength, jump reach and grip strength. Other abilities are also routinely measured, including senses such as hearing, sight, smell and touch. Designers rely heavily on anthropometric data when making decisions concerning the size, weight and shape of things. This is particularly important in areas such as the design of computer hardware and software, cars, furniture and domestic objects.

> *[If] 'people are made safer, more comfortable, more efficient, or just happier, the designer has succeeded.'*
> Henry Dreyfuss, early pioneer of ergonomics

Many designers and organisations have successfully adopted and extended ergonomic principles into their design work. A notable example is Emilio Ambasz's Vertebra chair (1977), which was the first office chair to respond automatically to the body's movement. It was developed almost entirely based on sound ergonomic principles. Another is Swedish company Ergonomi Design Gruppen, which bases its award-winning designs on the successful implementation of ergonomic knowledge into its products.

Jacob Jensen

Jacob Jensen is famous for his minimalist designs, which, for many years, were regarded as the ultimate in audio styling, setting the aesthetic standard for audio systems design worldwide.

Born 1926,
Copenhagen, Denmark
Importance Pioneer
of industrial design
in Scandinavia

Jensen is one of Scandinavia's most famous product designers. He trained as an industrial designer at the Applied Arts School in Copenhagen, before working as chief designer in Denmark's first industrial design practice, founded in 1949 by Sigvard Bernadotte and Acton Bjørn. During his time there (1952 to 1958) Jensen worked on a number of projects with Raymond Loewy in the US. He then spent two years in America himself, where he established a design office with Richard Latham and others, and taught at the University of Illinois, Chicago, before returning to Copenhagen to form his own industrial design consultancy.

Today, Jensen is best known for his work with Bang and Olufsen (B&O), and is widely regarded as one of the leading manufacturers of audio technology products. All of his designs for the company push the aesthetic, functional and user-centred boundaries in audio technology equipment. Jensen is renowned for his innovative approach to audio product design and the manner in which he resolves often challenging

and competing demands of the user and manufacturer alike. With his assistant, David Lewis, Jensen introduced the linear tuning system, inspired by the slide-rule, so that its appearance would suggest the ultimate in precision.

Jensen's B&O Beogram 1200 hi-fi system, with a radio, amplifiers, record player and tape recorder (1969) – perhaps his most successful product – was awarded a Danish industrial design prize for its harmonious balance between apparatus and furniture. He was also responsible for technical advances, such as the tangential pickup arm system, a method of playing vinyl records that since became standard, and which first appeared on the B&O Beogram 4000 record player (1972). Similarly, Jensen's work on the B&O Beolit 600 radio (1960) introduced a number of ergonomic advances over previous transistor radios by developing more simplified controls.

Since the late 1960s, Jensen has designed a succession of audio equipment for B&O, including the Beosystem 5500, a four-unit music system controlled via an infrared control panel and the Beocenter 9000 music system and CD player with touch-sensitive illuminated controls. His Beogram 1800 record player (1975) is notable for its extremely flat chassis of plastic and brushed aluminium.

Jensen has also designed a number of products for other Danish manufacturers such as a stainless-steel wristwatch for Georg Jensen (1967), the E76 push-button telephone for Alcatel-Kirk (1972), an office chair for Labofa (1979), ultrasound equipment for Bruel and Kjaer (1982) and a wristwatch for Max René (1983). He has won numerous design prizes for his work, including the German Award Die Gute Industrieform and the Industiral Designers Society of America (IDSA) prize. His work is included in the permanent collection of the Museum of Modern Art (MoMA), New York.

Dieter Rams

Dieter Rams is regularly described as the most important industrial designer of post-war Germany. As director of design at Braun, the German consumer electronics manufacturer, he developed and maintained a clear, strong visual language for all products. Today, Braun products are renowned for their elegant, legible and consistent forms, and their use of highly appropriate materials and restricted colour palette across the entire product range.

Born 1932, Wiesbaden, Germany
Importance One of the most important industrial designers of the post-war era; an exponent of 'good design'

Rams studied architecture and completed an apprenticeship in fine carpentry before working as an architect in Frankfurt, in 1955. At this time, he was working with the leading German modernist, Otto Appel, whose architectural office had links with the American practice Skidmore, Owings and Merrill. Rams claims that he was impressed by the 'can do' attitude of the American practice and learnt the simple essence of industrial construction while he was there. In 1961 he started working for Braun, where he became a product designer and, eventually, head of the design department.

Rams spent nearly 40 years at Braun, designing and developing a huge selection of products for industrial mass production on a large scale. Throughout this period, he

remained steadfastly committed to producing the best products in the world. His belief in good design led him to proclaim: 'I think that good designers must always be avant-gardists, always one step ahead of the times… they should question everything… they must have an intuition for people's changing attitudes.'

Many of Rams' Braun products have now become collectors' items, including the T1000 world receiver – the first all-wavelength portable radio, and the Phonosuper SK4 radio and record player, which he co-designed with Hans Gugelot. Nicknamed Snow White's Coffin on account of its being predominantly white, the SK4 marked a radical departure from the design conventions of the era. Here was a piece of technological equipment that was coveted as much for its appearance as for its function. It set a trend for years to come.

Much of Rams' design output is characterised by its pared-down rationalist aesthetic, which exemplifies his 10 tenets of good design.

> Good design is innovative.
> Good design makes a product useful.
> Good design is aesthetic.
> Good design helps us to understand a product.
> Good design is unobtrusive.
> Good design is honest.
> Good design has longevity.
> Good design is consequent down to the last detail.
> Good design is concerned with the environment.
> Good design is as little design as possible.

In 1968, Rams was elected an Honorary Designer for Industry by the Royal Society of Arts, London. To this day, he believes the main responsibility of designers is to instil order in contemporary life. He retired from Braun in 1995, but his design legacy continues to influence the philosophy of the company.

Ettore Sottsass

Ettore Sottsass was one of the most influential and important designers of the second half of the twentieth century. He was a key player in the postmodern design movement and was a founding member of the massively influential Memphis group (see page 32) in the early 1980s.

Born 1917, Innsbruck, Austria
Importance Champion of the avant-garde
Died 2007, Milan, Italy

Although trained as an architect, Sottsass secured a permanent place in pop culture with his designs of everyday items, including office cabinets, table lamps, ice buckets and silverware. He worked for several major manufacturers including the office equipment company Olivetti, the domestic products company Alessi, the furniture companies Knoll and Artemide, and the glass company Venini.

During his time at Olivetti, where he worked as a design consultant from 1958 to 1980, he created the Elea 9003 calculator and the popular portable red typewriter – the Valentine – released on Valentine's Day in 1969. Sottsass referred to his Valentine typewriter as the 'anti-machine machine'—it looks nothing like a piece of equipment you would expect to see in an office. The Valentine's features included a carriage that dropped to the level of the keyboard and a storage case, although it was the bright-red colour that Sottsass used that made it most memorable. In keeping with many designed products of the 1960s, the Valentine is made of bright-red injection-moulded ABS plastic.

Sottsass designed a number of chairs and other objects for the office environments of Olivetti. Like his Valentine typewriter, his 'Synthesis 45' office chair was made from brightly coloured yellow plastic and intended to appeal to a more youthful market. This chair was much envied and copied and it set new standards for office chairs with respect to ergonomic issues and comfort while challenging commonly held assumptions that office furniture had to be monochromatic.

Sottsass stood out because he rejected the prevailing modernist design principles, favouring involvement in the radical design movements of the 1960s and 1970s. It was at this point in his career that he found a number of like-minded designers to collaborate with in the form of both Studio Alchimia from the late 1970s, and Memphis during the 1980s. It is his design output during his time with Memphis that most people readily recall. Among his designs was the Seggiolina chair (1980), using plastic laminates and industrially produced components; and the Teodora chair (1986), which epitomises the Memphis design philosophy through its use of highly patterned textile plastic laminates.

Sottsass's work has been exhibited at major venues around the world for more than three decades and features prominently in the contemporary design collections of all major museums.

POP CULTURE
Short for popular culture, this term refers to the prevailing cultural elements within a population. It appears in many guises from art and design to film, music and television.

Richard Sapper

Widely described as the designer 'who has never produced a bad design', Richard Sapper is well-known for being one of the few designers ever to have lived, who is able to transfer successful and innovative solutions from one creative domain and use it in another one. A keen observer of the way that people go about their day-to-day lives, and operate within their valuably held traditions, Sapper is brilliant at negotiating the often conflicting demands of the consumer and the manufacturer in the realisation of exquisite designs.

Born 1932, Munich, Germany
Importance Designed one of the world's most recognised table lights ever produced

Sapper studied philosophy, anatomy, graphics, engineering and economics at Munich University. In 1956, he worked briefly in the design division at Mercedes Benz before going to Milan, where he worked with Alberto Rosselli and Gió Ponti. From 1958, he was employed in the practice of Marco Zanuso – a collaboration that continued well into the 1970s. One notable product to arise from their partnership was the compact Grillo telephone for Siemens in 1966.

In 1972, Richard Sapper designed the Tizio lamp for Artemide, an enormously successful high-tech task light, which has proved to be one of his most popular products. His understanding of engineering is evident in the design, which has now achieved iconic status.

The Tizio, Italian for 'what's-his-name', is made from aluminium and ABS plastic, and is held firmly to the work surface by the weight of the transformer in the base. The Tizio is a triumph of

'Thirty per cent of success is having the idea, seventy per cent is working with other people to make it a living product.'

technology and materials over form. The lamp incorporates ultra-thin, low-voltage halogen electrical wires, which are concealed within the Tizio's skinny structural members. The small reflector at the top of the lamp holds a powerful, small, and almost weightless bulb. The arms of the lamp articulate with little effort, about snap joints coloured in bright-red ABS plastic, which can be placed in a variety of different positions. Initially only available in black, Sapper claimed that he designed the Tizio table lamp because he could not find a work lamp that suited him – 'I wanted a small head and long arms; I didn't want to have to clamp the lamp to the desk because it's awkward. And I wanted to be able to move it easily.' Black, angled and minimalist, the Tizio lamp was a revolutionary design for its time and received massive critical and commercial success in the early 1980s, becoming an important feature of any young and successful executive's furnishings.

COMPASSO D'ORO
Established in Italy, in 1954, the Compasso d'Oro (Golden Compass) is an award given to acknowledge and promote high-quality industrial design of Italian origin.

In 1983 Richard Sapper designed the Bollitore three-tone whistling kettle for Alessi. This has also become a cult object, and is often referred to as the first designer kettle. It has been said that Sapper's design of the Bollitore was inspired by the steam ships and barges that pass up and down the River Rhine. His other notable designs for Alessi include the Cafetière coffee maker (1979) and the Uri Uri watch (1988).

Sapper has also acted as a design consultant to Fiat and Pirelli and, from 1980, IBM, where he designed their iconic ThinkPad among other IBM computers. He has designed furniture for Knoll, Unifor, Molteni and Castelli, and has won the Compasso d'Oro prize on numerous occasions.

MEMPHIS

Memphis was born on 11 December 1980, in the house of Italian designer, Ettore Sottsass. The group was christened Memphis when the Bob Dylan lyric 'stuck inside of mobile with the Memphis blues again' stuck repeatedly at 'Memphis blues again' on Sottsass' record player. From this informal gathering grew one of the most important periods in design of the twentieth century. Memphis would go on to shake the design world to its foundations during its short life, and is now credited with introducing postmodernism to the international arena.

Memphis had its roots in the experimental, radical and intellectual group, Studio Alchimia, formed in the late 1970s by Italian designers, Alessandro and Adriana Guerriero with Alessandro Mendini. The group's philosophy was based on the complete rejection of the objective and technical orientation of functionalism, which had been promoted by the modernists of the early twentieth century and had dominated design for the last 50 years. The group defined itself as a post-radical forum, whose main objective was to design and produce an entirely new, emotional and sensual relationship between everyday users and their products.

By 1981, Memphis had grown to include a number of well-respected designers including Andrea Branzi, Barbara Radice, Michele De Lucchi, Nathalie du Pasquier and George Sowden. Between them, they had completed over a hundred drawings of furniture, lighting and ceramics, reflecting a variety of influences including futuristic themes, past styles such as art deco and 1950s kitsch. Sottsass and his younger members were highly motivated and were hell bent on freeing themselves from what they saw as the tyranny of the prevailing, soulless, 'good design' of the period.

The members of Memphis exploited their extensive network of contacts and set their collaborative talents on producing a range of batch-produced designs, richly decorated in plastic laminates. Plastic laminates were not new, having made their way into people's homes years before on account of their practical and functional qualities. Memphis, however, turned this situation on its head by taking laminates from their usual hidden-away closets, bathroom and kitchen cabinets and incorporating them in designs for living-room tables, cabinets, chairs and couches – places where they would always be on view. Moreover, these plastic laminates were decorated with all manner of motifs such as Michele de Lucchi's brutal, geometric 'Micidial' and 'Fantastic' patterns. Comic strips, false venetian blinds, false serpents and even false painting masterpieces also featured in their designs. Some, such as Sottsass' 'Bacterio' and 'Spugnato', evoked neutral and organic forms.

Memphis quickly grabbed the attention of the international design scene, following its 1981 debut at the Salone del Mobile in Milan, with its new, postmodern, vocabulary of design. By the early 1980s, the group had extended its number to include an international array of designers such as Shiro Kuramata, Javier Mariscal, Masanori Umeda and Michael Graves. By the mid-1980s, however, Sottsass had become increasingly disillusioned with it and the media circus that followed it around. In 1985, he announced that he was leaving the collective, signalling the beginning of the end of what is now recognised as one of the most important design groups in the history of modern design.

Mario Bellini

Mario Bellini was a strong figure in the surge of Italian design in the international market between 1955 and 1965. During his time working for office equipment company

Born 1935, Milan, Italy
Importance World-renowned Italian product designer and architect

Olivetti, he was responsible for creating a new, formal design aesthetic for machines that had been absent in the pre-war period. His method of working was unusual in that he did not draw his designs, but communicated them directly to his model maker who interpreted them in three-dimensional prototypes.

Bellini studied architecture at the Milan Polytechnic until 1959. Between 1961 and 1963, he was director of design at the Italian department store chain La Rinascente, after which he moved to Olivetti, where he remained for many years as a chief design consultant, producing numerous calculator and typewriter models including the Divisumma 18/28 calculators (1973) and the Praxis 35 and Praxis 45 typewriters (1981).

Olivetti and Bellini shared a common respect for one another, and their positive working relationship saw Bellini given huge creative freedom in all of Olivetti's commercial projects. He had overall responsibility for the design of all Olivetti's office products, such as terminals, teleprinters and typewriters. Bellini's Divisumma 18 was a radical product, even by Olivetti's often far-reaching

'[I am] not interested in considering an object as an isolated item. It is part of a wider system of objects, structures and spaces, that work together as part of our environment as a whole.'

standards. Made of bright-yellow ABS plastic, the machine had a rubber covering, which made the gadget feel and look altogether softer and warmer. The design became an icon of the pop era.

In 1972, Bellini exhibited a mobile micro-living environment called Kar-a-Sutra, made in collaboration with Cassina, Citroën and Pirelli, at the exhibition 'Italy: The New Domestic Landscape', held at the Museum of Modern Art (MoMA), New York. Among his most notable furniture designs are the Amanta sofa (1966) and Le Bambole seating system (1972) for B&B Italia, and the Cab seating, a chair with a lightweight steel frame entirely covered in leather, (1977) for Cassina, and the Figura seating (1985), co-designed with Dieter Thiel, for the German Bundestag in Berlin. He has also designed lighting, electrical appliances and other utilitarian objects for companies such as Artemide, Brionvega, Bulthaupt, Flos, Minerva, Poltrona and Yamaha.

Bellini's work was often architecturally inspired, but he always focused on the 'human factor' elements of the products that he designed, believing that we can only truly improve the quality of our environment by 'moving towards a more anthropocentric view of man's environment, at least as far as disciplinary and didactic, or cultural, aspects are concerned'.

Alongside his rich design career, Bellini was a professor of design at the Institute of Industrial Design, Venice (1962 to 1965), and taught at the University of Applied Arts in Vienna from 1982 to 1983, and at the Domus Academy in Milan from 1986 to 1991. Between 1986 and 1991, he was editor-in-chief of the Italian design and architecture magazine *Domus*. His designs have won several prizes, including seven Compasso d'Oro awards (see page 31).

James Dyson

James Dyson is one of the most successful designers of the twentieth century, best known as the inventor of the Dyson DC01 Dual Cyclone bag-less vacuum cleaner, which works on the principle of cyclonic separation. The DC01 became the best-selling vacuum cleaner in the UK, with an amazing 32,000 units selling per month – five times that of its nearest competitor.

Born 1947, Cromer, England
Importance Invented a bag-less vacuum cleaner that works on the principle of cyclonic separation

Dyson attended the Byam Shaw School of Drawing and Painting in Kensington, London, before completing his design studies in furniture and interior design at the Royal College of Art, London. His first product, the Sea Truck, was launched in 1970, while he was still at the Royal College of Art, and amassed sales of around £300 million. The Sea Truck also won him a Design Council Award and the Duke of Edinburgh's special prize in 1975. Dyson went on to join the company Rotork in Bath, where he managed the new Marine Division until 1973, when he was appointed director.

A year later he decided to go it alone to develop his next product, the Ballbarrow – a modified version of a wheelbarrow using a ball to replace the wheel, and the Waterolla – a water-filled plastic garden roller. Dyson stayed with the idea of a ball, inventing the Trolleyball – a boat launcher with ball wheels

– and the Wheelboat, which could travel at speeds of 65 kmph (40mph) on land and water.

In 1979, Dyson sold his shares in the Ballbarrow to fund his explorations in new vacuum-cleaner technology and, over the next five years, he produced more than 5,000 prototypes, eventually resulting in the Dyson DC01 Dual Cyclone vacuum cleaner. Similar to the much larger cyclone towers used for removing hazardous particles from the atmosphere in saw mills and spray-paint booths, Dyson's idea to use a cyclonic method of suction – thus eliminating the need for a bag – resulted in a vacuum cleaner that provided a high level of constant suction. Although his first commercial vacuum cleaner, the pink and lilac G-Force (1983), was chosen for the cover of *Design* magazine, it failed to impress the established vacuum-cleaner manufacturers in the UK.

'Design is about how something works, not how it looks. It's what's inside that counts. The best designs are the result of someone's questioning everything around them.'

He decided to take the G-Force to Japan in 1985 where, six years later, having enjoyed remarkable success, it was awarded the International Design Fair prize. Japanese consumers adored the G-Force and it eventually achieved cult product status there, and news of the G-Force's success spread to other shores eventually.

Many of Dyson's designed products now feature in major galleries and exhibitions throughout the world. He has extended his range of vacuum cleaners to include many variations on his earlier cyclonic bag-less theme, which has resulted in his company gaining significant market share in the UK and other markets. Dyson has lately turned his attention to other problem products, such as the domestic washing machine and hand dryers in public toilets.

Ross Lovegrove

Lovegrove is one of a number of current designers whose mode of working crosses several disciplinary boundaries. Working often at the edges, intersections and beyond the boundaries of design, architecture, science and technology, he adopts a playful and experimental approach to the design work he undertakes.

Born 1958, Cardiff, Wales
Importance Combines a love of high tech with that of the natural world

Lovegrove commenced his design studies at Manchester Polytechnic before moving on to complete a master's degree in design at the Royal College of Art in 1983.

In 1990, he set up his own design practice, Studio X, having collaborated with Julian Brown on joint projects for several years. Since graduating, Lovegrove has worked with a number of blue-chip clients on a wide range of projects, such as personal music players for Sony, computers for Apple and furniture for Knoll International.

Along with several other architects and designers of his generation – Karim Rashid, Ron Arad and Will Alsop – Lovegrove is considered part of the recent 'blobject' movement in architecture and design. Moving away from the design concepts of conventional modernism, blobjects tend to have organic and amorphic forms. A blobject is, typically, any colourful, mass-produced, fluid, curvaceous form. The term, a conjunction of the words 'blobby' and 'object', was first coined by the design critic and educator, Steven Skov Holt, in the early 1990s. It encompasses anything from a typographic font to a piece of furniture, an article of clothing, a building or a piece of sculpture. Blobjects can be made of any material and in any size or scale for the home, office, car or outdoors. Most commonly, however, they are fabricated in plastic, metal and rubber in an attempt to give them a more organic feel. Advances in computer-aided design and manufacture (see page 124), information visualisation, rapid prototyping, materials and injection moulding have given designers the chance to use these new shapes and to explore transparency and translucency without significant extra production costs.

BIOMORPHISM
A term used to describe manufactured products, buildings and environments whose form has been influenced by living organisms.

Among those of Lovegrove's projects that can be described to have this 'blobject' aesthetic, are his packaging for Ty Nant water, his Solar Bud solar-powered garden lighting system for Luceplan, his visually Organic cutlery for Pottery Barn and his Eye digital camera for Olympus. Some of his designs reveal the strong influence of English sculptor Henry Moore, in terms of their smooth forms. Many of his designs are inspired and influenced by the natural world and informed by his wide-ranging understanding of human needs as well as an awareness of state-of-the-art materials and the latest cutting-edge manufacturing and production technologies.

Like many of his contemporary design colleagues, Lovegrove is well aware of the current ecological demands we face as a society. A lot of his work, therefore, attempts to reconcile environmental pressures with the demands of ever more discerning consumers. His carbon fibre and aluminium design pieces shown at the Endurance exhibition in New York, in 2007, illustrated very well the tensions between mass production and global sustainability.

Jonathan Ive

Jonathan Ive is widely regarded as one of the most important product designers of his generation, creating some of the most important products for Apple in recent times. Not many designers enjoy the commercial, cultural and critical success that Ive has achieved, who can rightly claim to have changed the way that millions of people work and play.

Born 1967, London, England
Importance His designs for Apple have revolutionised the way people use and think of computers and personal music players

Ive studied design at Newcastle Polytechnic (now Northumbria University) before co-founding Tangerine in 1990, a design consultancy, where he developed everything from power tools to televisions. He also did some work for Apple, and then joined the company full-time in 1992, at around the same time of Apple's founder Steve Jobs' departure. For a few years Apple suffered in terms of design and innovation, but when Jobs returned to the company, in 1997, and put Ive in charge of design, Apple's fortunes took a turn for the better.

Ive created the original iMac in 1998 and, with it, gave rise to an aura of desirability and emotion that, until then, had never been associated with computer products. The

'Right at the end of my time at college I discovered the Mac. I remember being astounded at just how much better it was than anything else I had tried to use... I had a sense of connection via the object with the designers.'

translucent machine, with its curvaceous organic form, broke all existing personal computer design rules. It looked amazing and, at its launch, it quickly became obvious that Apple had a commercial winner on its hands. Apple's market share before the iMac had shrunk to a disastrous three per cent in 1997; over the course of one weekend, however, an astounding 150,000 iMacs were sold.

As well as selling more than two million units in its first year, the iMac transformed the field of product design by introducing colour and lightness to a previously drab world, where practically all products were encased in opaque grey or beige plastic. Almost immediately, the iMac changed the currency of personal computer evaluation: quantitative measures of capacity and speed were given over to the more subjective measures of whether or not the machine looked warm and inviting. Helped by some very clever advertising campaigns, the machine became the best-selling computer in America, thanks to its radical design and not its technology.

The influence of the iMac on a wide range of other designed products has been overwhelming. Suddenly, a huge raft of brightly coloured, translucent products hit the shelves, aimed at satisfying the newly created aesthetic desires of consumers. Apple and Ive have continued to create a number of groundbreaking products, including the iPod, which has had a dramatic impact on the way that people consume and listen to music.

Michael Thonet

One of the first designers to embrace industrial manufacturing techniques, Michael Thonet is credited with producing one of the world's first, and most successful, industrially designed products - the Model No 14 bentwood chair. Still in production today, the design has remained unchanged for over 150 years.

Born 1796, Boppard, Germany
Importance Inventor and designer of bentwood furniture
Died 1871, Vienna, Austria

Having completed an apprenticeship in cabinetmaking, in 1819, Thonet started his own furniture-making company, Gebrüder Thonet, through which he became an early pioneer of modern industrial manufacturing techniques. In the early 1830s, he began to experiment with bending wood furniture components into curves, and he quickly patented a technique for bending wood under steam pressure.

Thonet's method involved soaking strips of wood in boiling glue, layering them, laminating them and pressing them into moulds to create curved forms for chairs, bed headboards and sofa armrests.

Thonet's Model No 14 bentwood chair was first seen in 1859, and contained approximately half a dozen components, which could be flat-packed for transportation and assembled easily on opening. The chair achieved Thonet's ultimate goal of designing a mass-produced chair and, by 1930, over 50 million units had been sold worldwide.

Thonet's remarkable success is due, largely, to his adherence to mechanised methods of production, which allowed him to sell his products at very competitive prices. In 1860, for example, the No 14 chair cost less to buy than a bottle of wine. Admired by many artists and designers of the period the No 14 chair, sometimes called the 'Bistro' or 'Vienna Café' chair, is now one of the most important chairs in furniture design history.

Thonet exhibited his furniture designs at an exhibition staged by the Koblenz Art Association in 1841. His work at this exhibition was deemed highly innovative and attracted the attention of the Austrian Chancellor Prince Metternich, who consequently invited Thonet to live and work in Vienna. Having secured the necessary financial backing, Thonet established a furniture workshop in Gumpendorf, Vienna, with his four sons, Franz, Michael, August and Joseph. Over the next couple of years, Thonet and his sons experimented with developing techniques for mass-producing furniture which included the process of steaming wood rods and placing them in metal moulds to dry. In 1851, Thonet exhibited his new furniture designs at the Great Exhibition in Hyde Park, London, where he was awarded a gold medal.

By the time of Thonet's death, in 1871, Gebrüder Thonet had established branches in the majority of all the major European cities as well as in Russia and the United States. Thonet Frères, a French subsidiary of Gebrüder Thonet, was created in 1929. This new French venture extended its furniture portfolio by moving into new territories such as the manufacture of progressive tubular steel furniture designed by the likes of Marcel Breuer, Ludwig Mies van der Rohe and Le Corbusier.

The company has been a key figure in many of the most significant developments in modern design. The likes of Josef Hoffmann, Otto Wagner and Adolf Loos, who all designed for Thonet at some time in their lives, and exploited Thonet's bentwood techniques to create iconic chair designs of their own, many of which are still in production today.

MODERNISM

Modernism was a dominant force in design, driven largely by a progressive and socially motivated ideology. It was not merely an important part of twentieth-century design, but a major cultural revolution, and one that transformed Western civilisation for ever.

The modernist movement grew out of the technological innovations of the nineteenth century and the moral crusades of design reformers such as A W N Pugin, John Ruskin and William Morris. Such people set about reforming design through their ideas of supremacy of utility, simplicity and appropriateness over luxury, in an attempt to rid society of what they saw as the corruption, greed and decadence of the prevailing high-Victorian style. William Morris believed that it was the moral responsibility of both designers and manufacturers to produce objects of quality, and that design could, and should, be used as a democratic tool for social change. His ideas went on to have a fundamental impact on the development of the modern movement in Europe.

At the start of the twentieth century, a number of craft-based guilds and workshops opened throughout western Europe and North America, which shared the view that machines and industrial processes could be used as the means to achieve real social reform. Formed in 1907, the Deutscher Werkbund was the first organisation to put such a theory into practice. Superfluous decoration was removed and improved standardisation was achieved, in turn increasing efficiency in production and material usage, benefitting both consumer and producer.

Modernism provided a universal design language that was aimed at being impervious to fashion. Adolf Loos' famous 1908 publication, *Ornament und Verbrechen* (*Ornament and Crime*), and the slightly later publication, *Form ohne Ornament* (*Form without Ornament*), linked unnecessary decoration to the debasing of society and extolled the virtues of rational design for production.

As the twentieth century began, pioneers of the modern movement wanted to create buildings and products that expressed the spirit of a new age. Collectively, they felt that nineteenth-century architecture and design borrowed far too heavily from the past, and was usually either oppressively bound to past styles or annoyingly picturesque. Architects including Josef Hoffmann in Austria and Le Corbusier in France wished to create a machine aesthetic that celebrated the accuracy and energy of the emerging technologies. It was not long before the concept was adopted by all areas of design. The result was an exciting marriage of the relatively new techniques and materials of mass production with the pared back designs of modernist crusaders. Highlights from this period include the furniture and metalware designs emerging from Josef Hoffman's Wiener Werkstätte (see page 86) and the Bauhaus school of design (see page 90).

The modern movement gained momentum after the Second World War, when its theories were influential in the planning and rebuilding of several major European and North American cities. Architectural projects of note during this time include Charles Rennie Mackintosh's highly decorated buildings in Glasgow, Scotland, and Frank Lloyd Wright's flowing interior spaces and projecting roofs in the United States. Later masterpieces of modernism were created by the likes of Le Corbusier and Peter Behrens. Arguably the greatest example of modernism ever created is the Seagram Building, in New York City, designed by Ludwig Mies van der Rohe in 1954.

Charles Rennie Mackintosh

Architect, designer and artist Charles Rennie Mackintosh is celebrated around the world as one of the most creative figures of the early twentieth century. Influenced by the aesthetics of the English Gothic and the Far East, his contribution to modern architecture and design is unquestioned.

Born 1868, Glasgow, Scotland
Importance A major exponent of the modern movement in Scotland
Died 1928, London, England

Mackintosh studied at the Glasgow School of Art in 1883 and, the next year, was apprenticed to John Hutchison, a local architect in Glasgow, where he began a five-year pupilage. In 1889, he joined Honeyman and Keppie architects in Glasgow as a draughtsman, where he received a traditional Beaux Arts training typical of the period. In 1896 Francis Newbery, the inspirational director of Glasgow School of Art, invited 12 local architects to enter a competition to design a new building for the school. One of the firms was Honeyman and Keppie. The firm won the competition, with Mackintosh as designer, and this commission was to seal his reputation. The art school's first phase was completed in 1899, but it was the completion of the second phase, in 1907, and the library extension (1907 to 1909) that made his name.

Among Mackintosh's closest friends were J Herbert MacNair, a colleague at Honeyman and Keppie, and the sisters Margaret and Frances Macdonald, whom he had met at Glasgow School of Art. Working both independently and collaboratively, they became one of the era's dominant forces of modern design. Known as 'The Four', they created some of the most innovative and provocative graphic and decorative art designs of the period. Their work was exhibited in Liege, Paris, London, Venice and elsewhere, and notably published in *The Studio* magazine and *The Yellow Book*. This attention helped to mark

Glasgow as a distinctive artistic centre, and contributed to the recognition of a 'Glasgow Style' of decorative and interior design.

Mackintosh's work had a significant impact on the Vienna Workshop, Hermann Muthesius and the Deutsche Werkbund. He created many of the best known and most influential buildings, furniture and decorative schemes of the early twentieth century. Mackintosh was an architect who designed schools, offices, churches, tearooms and homes, an interior designer and decorator, an exhibition designer, a designer of furniture, metalwork, textiles and stained glass and, in later years, focused entirely on watercolour painting.

His masterpiece, the Glasgow School of Art, the country estate house Windy Hill at Kilmacolm, the Hill House, Helensburgh, Scotland Street School, and a series of city-centre tea-room interiors are counted among his architectural triumphs. In common with many of his contemporaries, Mackintosh believed that the architect was

responsible not just for the fabric of a building, but for every detail of its interior design. He was one of the most sophisticated exponents of the theory of the room as a work of art, and created highly distinctive furniture of great formal sophistication. Many of his pieces are, today, considered among the moden classics.

Carlo Bugatti

Bugatti worked in architecture, interiors, ceramics, paintings, silverware and textiles but was best known for his furniture. Betraying Gothic, Moorish and Oriental influences, his style was highly individualistic, producing extreme examples of the artistically extravagant and his furniture, in particular, assumed completely new and astounding shapes and ornamentation. He is generally regarded as a special case in art nouveau and is often compared with Antoni Gaudí in that both of them are seen as outsiders.

Born 1856, Milan, Italy
Importance
Extravagant art nouveau designer
Died 1940, Molsheim, France

Bugatti was a student at both the Academy of Fine Arts of Brera, Milan and at the Ecole des Beaux-Arts, Paris. Having originally trained in the fine arts, as a painter and sculptor, his career in furniture design began when he made a number of pieces of furniture for his sister Luiga's wedding to the artist Giovanni Segantini, in 1880. He rose quickly in the design world and, by 1888, had built up his own cabinetmaking and decorating company, based in Milan. His output of interior designs, furniture and silverware was prodigious and it appears that his work was highly regarded during this time. In 1900, he won a silver medal for the work that he exhibited at the Exposition Universelle in Paris. Later that same year, he created a series of designs for the Khedive's palace in Istanbul, and he also completed an interior-design scheme for Cyril Flowers, the first Lord Battersea, in London.

Bugatti is generally considered something of an outsider in the annals of design history. His creative output falls during the art nouveau period and he is often considered alongside other significant architects and designers of that time such as Antoni Gaudí, Victor Horta and Emile Gallé. Bugatti's work, however, is usually viewed as an extreme version of the style. His furniture designs, for example, assumed completely radical forms and were often highly decorated with ornaments from oriental odds and ends. Arguably his most successful piece of work was the Cobra chair. This was particularly innovative in the way its form utilised a single, continuous curve, elaborately covered in vellum and adorned with stylised flowers, dragonflies and geometric shapes. It was designed for the Snail Room at the first Exposizione Internazionale d'Arte Decorativa Moderna, Turin, Italy that was held in May 1902.

Bugatti often employed unusual materials for the time in his designs such as copper, ivory and vellum. Most of his work was created for his very wealthy patrons, which was also true of many of his contemporaries. Bugatti's furniture, like much of Gaudí's architecture, was considered too revolutionary for most, and around the beginning of the First World War their work fell out of favour, as did the art nouveau style in general. Today, however, Bugatti's exotic designs are considered eccentric enough to ensure him a place in design history. And the Bugatti name lives on: both of his sons inherited his creative traits – with Ettore designing luxury performance cars and Rembrandt emerging as an accomplished sculptor.

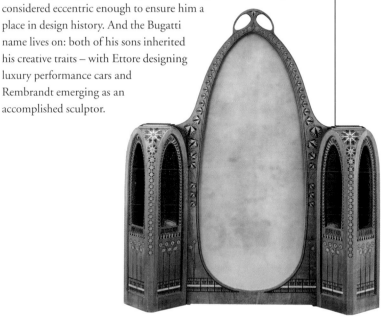

Furniture

Eileen Gray

Eileen Gray was one of the leading designers working in Paris after the First World War. She popularised and perfected the art of lacquered furnishings, her preference for its meticulous finish revealing a penchant for out-of-the-ordinary materials, in particular those used in Japanese decorative arts.

Born 1878, Enniscorthy, Ireland
Importance Irish furniture designer and architect: pioneer of the modern movement
Died 1976, Paris, France

Gray studied at the Slade School of Fine Art, London, from 1898 to 1902, before moving to Paris in 1907 with two fellow graduates. She then carried on her studies at the Académie Julian and the École Colarossi. Over the course of the next four years, Gray learnt oriental lacquering techniques from the Japanese craftsman Seizo Sugawara. Around 1910, she began designing lacquered screens and panels with figurative motifs, exhibiting at the Salon des Artistes Décorateurs, where her work was brought to the attention of the art collector Jacques Doucet. He became her first major client and she completed a number of products for him, including the Le Destin four-panel screen (1914) and the Lotus table (1915). Gray produced another example of the Le Destin screen as well as other furniture, including a wonderful daybed, named Pergola, for another client, Suzanne Talbot.

'To create, one must first question everything.'

Gray returned to Paris in 1917, two years after living in London (having left during the outbreak of the First World War), and started to design a range of furniture and accessories that included carpets, curtains and individual items of furniture in the French decorative style of the period. Around this time she completed her first major interior design project – the Rue de Lota apartment of Mme Mathieu

Lévy, which included her now-famous lacquered Block screens. In 1922, having already completed many one-off art deco commissions for wealthy clients, Gray opened her own shop, the Galerie Jéan Desert at 217 Rue du Faubourg Saint-Honoré, to exhibit and sell her work. She developed her own distinctive design style, which was influenced by the pure geometric forms of De Stijl but comprising something of an opulent twist, making use of industrially produced materials previously adopted by designers such as Mies van der Rohe and Le Corbusier. Her sumptuous Bibendum leather and tubular steel chair is now widely considered a design icon.

Gray's design work found a valuable admirer in the 1970s (when she was in her 90s), in the figure of the American collector Robert Walker, who sparked something of a major revival of interest in her work and which led to some of her designs being mass-produced. Somewhat overlooked by the design world until this time, Gray is now viewed as an important and influential designer of the early twentieth century. In 1972, she was selected as a Royal Designer to Industry by the Royal Society of Art in London for her services to design. Later, in 1978, her critically acclaimed Adjustable Table E 1027 was included in the permanent collection of the Museum of Modern Art in New York.

Gray remained powerfully independent throughout her career when the majority of other designers were linked in some way to one group or another such as De Stijl in the Netherlands. She also managed to carve a successful career during a time when most designers were male. Best known for her highly unique furniture and interior design work, Gray also managed to complete nine buildings during her career.

Gerrit Rietveld

Gerrit Thomas Rietveld was one of the most innovative furniture and interior designers of the twentieth century and a leading figure of the modern movement in Europe.

Born 1888, Utrecht, the Netherlands
Importance Dutch modernist designer, whose designs incorporated simple forms and primary colours
Died 1964, Utrecht, the Netherlands

Becoming one of the first members of the De Stijl group in 1919, Rietveld's Red Blue Chair came to epitomise the radical manifesto of this influential art and design movement.

Rietveld was born in Utrecht, the Netherlands, and lived and worked there all his life. He learned cabinetmaking from his father with whom he worked between the ages of 12 to 15. After leaving the family workshop, he trained as a draughtsman at the C J A Begeer goldsmith workshops, before qualifying as an architect in 1919.

Around this time, Rietveld was drawing largely on stylistic influences from Charles Rennie Mackintosh and Frank Lloyd Wright among others, but towards the middle of the decade he began to experiment more with abstract forms and shapes in his work. His most important architectural work, the Schroder House in Utrecht (1924 to 1925), connects closely with his furniture designs and the rigorous geometry and open-plan layout of this space, highlighted occasionally with bright panels of primary colours, created a completely new modernist aesthetic.

Rietveld's famous Red Blue Chair was designed in 1918 and was instantly heralded as being completely unique. He manipulated rectilinear volumes and examined the interaction of vertical and horizontal planes in much the same way as he did with his architecture. The striking use of primary colours with black are reminiscent of the De Stijl group and one of its most famous theorists in particular, Piet Mondrian. Although the chair was designed in 1918, the application of the red, yellow and blue paint was not added until 1923. His other famous piece of furniture, the Zig-Zag chair was created in 1934, manufactured from four single rectangular sections of hardwood, dovetailed, glued and fastened together. A demonstration of Rietveld's cabinetmaking expertise, the chair is one of the best examples of pure modernist seating ever designed.

> '[The] design must be able to stand freely and brightly on its own two feet, and the form must triumph over the material.'
>
> Rietveld on the Red Blue Chair

Over the years Rietveld's designs were shown in several groundbreaking exhibitions including those curated by De Stijl, as well as the Viennese Werkbund of 1931 and the Venice Biennial of 1954. A founding member of the Congrès Internationaux d'Architecture Moderne (CIAM), he also taught at a number of universities between 1942 and 1948 in the Netherlands and abroad. He was nominated an honorary member of the Bond van Nederlandse Architecten in 1963 and, in 1964, he was awarded an honorary degree from the Technische Hochschule in Delft.

Le Corbusier

Despite having little formal training, Le Corbusier is commonly thought of as one of the most important and admired architects and designers of the twentieth century.

Born 1887, La Chaux-de-Fonds, Switzerland
Importance
Groundbreaking modernist designer, architect and urban planner
Died 1965, Roquebrune-Cap-Martin, France

Le Corbusier, born Charles-Edouard Jeanneret, studied metal engraving at the School of Applied Arts at La Chaux-de-Fonds, Switzerland. While there, he was encouraged by his teacher, Charles L'Eplattenier, to take up architecture. In 1908, Jeanneret began an apprenticeship with Auguste Perret, who had earlier developed the application of reinforced concrete in his work. Jeanneret then went on to work for one year with Peter Behrens who shared his work ethos of function over style. Jeanneret's passion for logical, mass-produced designs culminated in his critically acclaimed Maison Dom-ino housing plans of 1915. These flexible, mass-produced houses employed the reinforced-concrete technique that he had used in past projects with Perret and Behrens.

In 1917 Jeanneret moved to Paris, and it was around this time that he adopted the moniker 'Le Corbusier'. For the

next couple of years he was editor-in-chief of the journal *L'Esprit Nouveau* and wrote several articles on subjects ranging from classical Greek architecture to his theories on the house as 'a machine for living'. These influential essays ultimately contributed significantly to the book entitled *Vers une Architecture* (*Towards a New Architecture*) in 1923. This book is still one of the best-selling architecture books of all time.

The majority of Le Corbusier's work throughout the 1920s and 1930s proposed a new visual clarity, which epitomised the International Style of the period, and for this he is widely acknowledged as one of the co-founders of purism. It was during this period that Le Corbusier produced some of his best architectural work, including his famous Villa Savoye in Poissy (1928 to 1929), Maison de Refuge, Paris (1930 to 1933) and his utopian La Ville Radieuse city plan of 1935.

By the 1950s, however, Le Corbusier had moved away from the formalism of the International Style towards a freer and more expressive exploration of the potential of concrete in his work, as demonstrated, for instance, in the roof of his Unité d'Habitation housing scheme, Marseilles (1946 to 1952) and in his outstanding Notre Dame du Haut church at Ronchamp (1950 to 1955). Together with his architect cousin, Pierre Jeanneret, and Charlotte Perriand, Le Corbusier also created a number of furniture pieces that have become modern-day design classics, such as the Model No B306 chaise longue for Thonet and Embru (1928) and the Model No LC2 Grand Confort club chair for Thonet (1928). Each had a pure, industrial aesthetic and relied on using the minimum of components in construction – in particular the tubular steel pioneered by Marcel Breuer of the Bauhaus (see page 90), paired with leather.

Le Corbusier's advancement of geometric formalism had widespread results, which led to the likes of his Pavillon de L'Esprit Nouveau for the 1925 'Exposition Internationale des Arts Décoratifs et Industriels Modernes' and the church at Ronchamp (1950 to 1955), now considered among his most important designs.

Marcel Breuer

Marcel Breuer is considered one of the early twentieth-century's most influential furniture designers, and is particularly renowned for introducing tubular steel to the world of furniture design. His Wassily chair (1925), made from extruded, nickel-plated tubular steel – ideal for mass production – was immediately hailed an important breakthrough in modern furniture design. It has been much copied and is still in production after more than 80 years.

Born 1902, Pécs, Hungary
Importance Pioneered the use of extruded tubular steel in furniture design
Died 1981, New York, United States

Breuer became one of the first apprentices to join the new furniture workshop at the Bauhaus (see page 90) in the summer of 1921. His first piece was the hand-carved and painted Romantic chair (also known as the African chair). By 1923, his work – most notably the Wood Slatted chair – was increasingly influenced by the abstract aesthetic of De Stijl, the Dutch art movement. Although firmly established as one of the most prolific members of the Bauhaus, and a protégé of its director, Walter Gropius, Breuer had little time for the intellectual debates that enveloped the rest of the school, preferring to design 'without having to philosophise before every move'.

From 1925 to 1928, Breuer ran the furniture workshop at the new Bauhaus in Dessau, and it was while teaching here that he investigated the use of tubular steel in furniture design, a material that offered affordability, hygiene, resilience and comfort without the need for springing. The concept had occurred to him while riding a bicycle: if tubular steel could be bent to form handlebars, he thought, why not bend it to make a furniture frame. His first tubular-metal chair was the 1925 B3 chair (later renamed the Wassily, after the Bauhaus teacher Wassily Kandinsky). Made from extruded nickel-plated tubular steel, the chair was unusually light and easy to assemble from ready-made steel tubes. The design defied gravity: the chair seemed to hover above the surface of the floor, enveloping the sitter in its low, deep seat.

> *'My most extreme work… the least artistic, the most logical, the least "cosy" and the most mechanical.'*
> Breuer on the Wassily chair

Within a year, designers everywhere were experimenting with tubular steel, taking furniture design into a completely different direction. Breuer, himself, went on to design a whole range of tubular-metal furniture including chairs, stools, tables and cupboards.

In 1935, Marcel Breuer emigrated to London to escape Nazi persecution on account of his Hungarian-Jewish origins. He stayed in London for a couple of years, during which time he produced a number of plywood furniture designs for the design company Isokon. Walter Gropius offered him a professorship at Harvard University's School of Design in Massachusetts and the pair collaborated together on a number of architecture projects. By 1946, Marcel Breuer had relocated to New York, where he continued to work on a number of architecture projects such as his magnificent 'concrete sculpture', the Whitney Museum of American Art in New York.

One of the leading figures of the modern movement, the lasting appeal of Breuer's design work is testament to his masterful grasp of aesthetics, manufacturing and production methods.

POSTMODERNISM

**Postmodernism has roots in the 1960s, when several
rebellious design movements were emerging, most notably
in Italy, such as the anti-design and radical design groups
Archizoom, Superstudio and Gruppo Strum. This was a decade
of rebellion in many spheres, not least design, where the likes
of Ettore Sottsass, Michael Graves, Alessandro Mendini,
Robert Venturi and Charles Jencks started to produce work
that made ironic comments on modern design.**

It wasn't until the early 1970s, on publication of *Learning from Las
Vegas,* written by Robert Venturi, Denise Scott Brown and Steven
Izenour, that the cultural honesty of the architectural commercialism
found in the desert city was deemed more relevant for modern society.
Postmodernists argued that modern architecture was completely
meaningless owing to its adherence of abstract geometry and denial of
ornamentation. They believed that any building that denied
ornamentation and symbolism basically portrayed architecture and
design as dehumanising and alienating. Postmodern designers declared
that decoration was respectable, one could be eclectic with integrity, and
that the entire history of architecture and design was there to be drawn
from. Postmodern designers dipped into classical furniture and swept
the history books of the baroque, ancient Egypt, and twentieth-century
kitsch and applied the results liberally to their creations.

Since the mid-1970s, a number of architects and designers have
experimented along postmodern lines, embracing a wide range of
cultural emblems from contemporary society that transcend
geographical boundaries. Forms and symbols were usually drawn
from past decorative styles such as classicism, art deco and
deconstructivism, but they also used imagery from significant
historical moments in art, such as surrealism.

Notable postmodern architects and designers include Michael Graves, Ettore Sottsass, Andrea Branzi, Aldo Rossi, George Sowden and Matteo Thun. These designers, and others, contributed significantly to the appeal and success of the movement, through their work in ceramics, textiles, furniture, lighting and architectural design. Major manufacturers of postmodern designs include Alessi, Artemide, Cassina, Formica and Draenert.

In Italy during the 1980s, postmodern work conducted under the umbrella groups of Studio Alchimia and Memphis (see page 32) began to receive international acclaim for the way that they assembled ironic comments on modernism through the application of applied decoration in their product and building proposals. The anti-design movements of the 1980s generally mocked the concept of 'good taste' through their use of bold-patterned plastic laminates and idiosyncratic forms and, at the same time, helped establish postmodernism as a true international style of the period. Postmodernism, in many ways, reflected the rise of individualism during the 1980s, and also the fragmented nature of most modern societies during this time. It was embraced by the high-earning, fast-living consumers of what has been referred to as 'wild' decade.

Much postmodern design has been dismissed as no more than 'an affair of the elite' according to Hans Hollein (himself a notable figure in postmodern design), and as the global recession of the early 1990s gripped most Western countries, the highly expressive, and occasionally irrational design approaches of postmodern designers began to fall out of favour with consumers.

Less is More

Ludwig Mies van der Rohe

Along with Le Corbusier and Frank Lloyd Wright, Ludwig Mies van der Rohe is seen as one of the twentieth-century's three most influential architects. His strict adherence to the the modern movement, laid down in some fundamental rules of beauty in design, resulted in his classic, and famous, Barcelona chair.

Born 1886, Aachen, Germany
Importance Pioneer of modern architecture and furniture design
Died 1969, Chicago, Illinois, United States

Mies van der Rohe – often referred to as Mies – first trained as a builder and, between 1900 and 1904, worked as a draughtsman of stucco ornaments for a local architect in Aachen, Germany. At the age of 19, and without any formal design training, he moved to Berlin (1905), where he worked for furniture designer Bruno Paul (until 1907), and subsequently joined the design practice of Peter Behrens (1908). During his time here, he worked alongside the likes of Walter Gropius, Hannes Meyer and Le Corbusier. He also created his first designs for high-rise glass buildings.

Mies opened his own studio in Berlin in 1912, but his career was interrupted by the events of the First World War. In 1919, he began to direct the architectural section of the Novembergruppe, a group dedicated to the revitalisation of the arts and architecture in Germany. During the 1920s, the majority of his architectural designs were speculative and experimental proposals for towering glass and steel structures. However, his furniture designs including the MR10 chair and the MR20 armchair were put into production by Berliner Metallgewerbe Joseph Müller between 1927 and 1931 and by the Bamberger Metallwerkstätten from 1931.

In 1929, Mies designed one of his most famous buildings, the German pavilion at the World Exhibition in Barcelona. Although a temporary structure, the Barcelona pavilion has become one of the most influential buildings in history. The pavilion has a flat roof supported by columns, while the pavilion's internal walls are made of glass and marble and can be moved around. Mies's concept of fluid space with a seamless flow between indoors and outdoors was further explored in several of his other projects.

Mies designed his celebrated twentieth-century design icon the Barcelona chair for use in the pavilion. Constructed from flat strips of chromed steel, welded together by hand, with leather upholstery, the chair achieves the calmness of line and the refinement of proportion and materials that are recognised traits of van der Rohe's architecture. It is an opulent, yet modern, interpretation of the *sella curulis* – a Roman magistrate's stool. Although only two were manufactured for the German Pavilion, the chair was so well received by the press and public that it immediately went into production.

Having emigrated to the United States in 1937, Mies was well established professionally by the 1940s and went on to design many famous buildings, including Farnsworth House, Illinois (1946 to 1950), one of the most radically minimalist houses ever designed, and his masterpiece, the famous 37-storey bronze and glass Seagram Building in New York (1954 to 1958), which he designed with assistance from Philip Johnson, and which is considered the most subtle development of the glass-walled skyscraper ever built.

As a designer both of furniture and buildings, Mies carried rationalism and functionalism to their ultimate stage of development. His famous dictum 'less is more' crystallised the basic philosophy of mid twentieth-century architectural design.

Alvar Aalto

One of the central figures of twentieth-century architecture and design, Alvar Aalto helped define modern architecture in Finland with his numerous public and private buildings.

Born 1898, Kuortane, Finland
Importance
Pioneer modernism in Scandinavian architecture and design
Died 1976, Helsinki, Finland

A central figure in international modernism, he was a pioneering and highly influential architect, with a phenomenal output of design work. He was also a significant and internationally respected designer of furniture, choosing wood as his main medium, but seeking constantly to design for mass production.

Between 1916 and 1921, Aalto studied at the Helsinki University of Technology. Over the next couple of years, he worked as an exhibition designer before setting up his own architectural office in Jyväskyla in 1923, which he later relocated to Turku, in 1927, and then finally on to Helsinki in 1933. His success as an architect owes much to his ability to integrate the traditional with the modern. He admired the classical architecture of ancient Greece and Rome, and was obsessed with the idea of architecture being close to nature, but also sought inspiration from the International Style that was prevalent in Europe at the time.

Among his early significant buildings were the Viipuri Library (1927 to 1935) and the Paimio Tuberculosis Sanatorium (1929 to 1933). He also created the Finnish Exhibition at the New York World's Fair in 1939. Other important Aalto buildings include the Villa Mairea, Noormarkku (1938 to 1939), the Baker Dormitory at the Massachusetts Institute of Technology (MIT, 1946 to 1947), and the Town Hall at Säynatsälo, Finland (1949 to 1952). At the MIT, he held the position of Professor of Architecture from 1946 to 1948, and was the Academy of Finland president from 1963 to 1968.

Aalto's innovative chair designs of the 1930s were the culmination of many years of experimenting with bending laminated wood, veneer bonding and moulding plywood. His experiments resulted in two of the world's most technically advanced chairs for the time, the Model No 41 (1932) and the cantilevered Model No 31 (1932), both of which were designed concurrently as part of the Paimio Tuberculosis Sanatorium project. Aalto's bent-plywood chairs influenced a generation of designers including Marcel Breuer and Charles and Ray Eames. The commercial success of his furniture designs allowed him and his wife, the designer Aino Marsio (1894–1949), to found the manufacturing company Artek in 1935.

Aalto's career spanned the birth and growth of modern architecture but, while he adopted from, and influenced, the new movement, he retained – and was greatly respected for – his own distinctive style. During his career, Aalto won a number of design awards including Gold Medals from the Royal Institute of British Architects and the American Institute of Architecture. The Museum of Modern Art (MoMA) in New York celebrated Aalto's life and work in three exhibitions in 1938, 1984 and 1997.

Arne Jacobsen

The Danish architect and designer, Arne Jacobsen, was one of the most important representatives of functionalism in the 1930s and 1950s, working in Copenhagen as a city planner, architect and designer. More recently, he has been credited with being the most important Danish architect and designer of the twentieth century.

Born 1902, Copenhagen, Denmark
Importance Pioneer of Danish modern design style
Died 1971, Copenhagen, Denmark

Originally, Jacobsen trained as a stonemason before commencing his studies at the Royal College of Art, Copenhagen. He graduated in 1927 and, in 1928, he received the Academy of Arts gold medal. Prior to this, however, at the 1925 Paris Exposition Internationale des Arts Décoratifs, he won the first of numerous honours when, at just 23 years of age, he was awarded the silver medal.

Jacobsen's first architectural milestone came when he won a design competition for the 'House of the Future' with Flemming Lassen in 1929, two years after graduating. This event marked the beginning of a long and versatile career for Jacobsen, who was interested in the idea of 'total design'. He worked on all elements in the architectural process, from textiles and sculptural furnishings to light fittings, ashtrays and cutlery. Jacobsen took on significant architectural projects for the Bella Vista housing project, Copenhagen (1930 to 1934), the SAS Air Terminal and Royal Hotel, Copenhagen (1956 to 1960), and St Catherine's College, Oxford (1960). The last is regarded as one of his masterpieces because of the way it adapts to its historical context.

Jacobsen is responsible for two of the most commercially and critically successful pieces of furniture design ever produced: his iconic side chair, popularly known as the Ant chair (1951), and the legendary Series 7, Model No 3107 chair (1955). Even today, both are considered almost perfect solutions for a contemporary lifestyle and, given that they were designed to meet the needs of domestic dwellings in the 1950s, this is a truly remarkable feat. Their success owes much to their lightweight construction, their compact nature and their timeless aesthetic.

Jacobsen also designed a number of very successful home wares, including lighting for Louis Poulsen, metalware for Stelton, textiles for August Millech and bathroom accessories for I.P. Lunds. His Cylinda range of tableware was awarded the ID prize in 1967 by the Danish Society of Industrial Design, and the International Design Award in 1968 by the American Institute of Interior Designers. He went on to become a professor at the Art Academy, and received honorary doctorates from a number of foreign universities and academies such as Oxford University.

Jacobsen's talents ran from architecture to the design of a wide range of goods including cutlery, carpets and light fittings but he remains best known for his furniture. Elegant, biomorphic forms characterise his chair designs, an aesthetic that is best seen in the three-legged Ant chair, more than five million of which have been produced since its design in 1951, making it one of the most successful chairs in the history of furniture design.

Hans Wegner

During the second half of the twentieth century, Hans Wegner established himself internationally as a designer of exquisitely balanced and beautifully crafted chairs, with over 500 designs to his name. Among them, the Chinese chair (1944) and the Round chair (1949) became archetypes for many of his later chairs. In 1950, the American magazine, *Interiors*, featured the Round chair on its cover and proclaimed it to be 'the world's most beautiful chair'.

Born 1914, Tønder, Denmark
Importance Denmark's most acclaimed chair designer
Died 2007, Copenhagen, Denmark

Hans Wegner trained as a carpenter in H F Stahlberg's workshop before studying at the Teknologisk Institut, Copenhagen, from 1936 to 1938, returning later as a tutor. In 1938, he accepted a position working with architects, Erik Møller and Flemming Lassen, in Arhus, before going on to start work as a furniture designer for Arne Jacobsen and Erik Møller on their design for Arhus Town Hall, in 1940. During this time, Wegner contributed furniture designs to a number of architectural projects. Between 1943 and 1946, he set up his own design office in Arhus before going on, in 1946, to work with Palle Suenson's architectural office in Copenhagen.

By the 1950s, Wegner had become one of the most important designers in Scandinavia, his Round chair having propelled him into international stardom. Arguably his most famous piece of work, a mark of the chair's significance is the fact that, years later, it became known simply as 'the chair' or 'the classic chair' and it even made a high-profile appearance during the televised 1961 presidential debates between Richard Nixon and John F Kennedy. Wegner himself has described the Danish design style of furniture as a 'continuous process of purification'.

Among Wegner's other critically acclaimed designs are the Peacock chair (1947), influenced by the traditional Windsor chair and featuring a unique, fanned backrest that evoked a bird's plume, the Y-chair (1950) and the Valet chair (1953). The last was a novel facility for storing a man's suit and had a backrest that could be used as a coat hanger, while the hinged seat lifted to reveal storage space for other items of clothing. Wegner's chair designs have, over the years, been manufactured by the likes of Fritz Hansen, A P Stolen, Johannes Hansen and P P Møbler.

Wegner is renowned for the manner in which his furniture designs blend a variety of natural materials, and he has been the recipient of a number of major international honours, including the Lunning Prize in 1951, the Prince Eugen medal in Sweden, the Danish Eckersberg medal, and the Grand Prix of the Milan Triennial (see page 21) in 1951. He received an Honorary Royal Designers for Industry in 1959 from the Royal Society of Arts, London; a Citations of Merit, from the Pratt Institute, New York, in 1959; and the International Design Award, New York, 1957. The Royal College of Art awarded Wegner an Honorary Doctorate in 1997. The Museum of Modern Art (MoMA) in New York and the Die Neue Sammlung in Munich are just two of more than 20 major museum collections throughout the world that showcase Wegner's furniture designs.

Pioneers of Moulded Fibreglass
Charles and Ray Eames

Charles and Ray Eames were jointly responsible for designing some of the most important pieces of twentieth-century furniture. Their mission – 'to get the most of the best, to the greatest number of people, for the least' had an enormous impact on twentieth-century design practice. Their achievements continue to be held in the highest regard today, as they are increasingly recognised as having single-handedly changed the course of modern design.

Born (Charles) 1907, St Louis, Missouri, United States; (Ray) 1912, Sacramento, California, United States
Importance Designed some of the most iconic furniture of the twentieth century
Died (Charles) 1978, St Louis, Missouri, United States; (Ray) 1988, Los Angeles, California, United States

Charles Eames, born in St Louis, Missouri, developed a deep interest in engineering and architecture during his senior school years. After high school, he was awarded an architecture scholarship to study at Washington University, in St Louis. He established his own architectural office in 1930 and began pushing the boundaries of his design ideas beyond the single discipline of architecture. He was awarded a fellowship to the Cranbrook Academy of Art in Michigan, where he cemented his friendship with Eliel Saarinen and his son Eero, and developed new partnerships, most notably with designers such as Harry Bertoia and, later, Ray Kaiser.

Born Bernice Alexandra Kaiser in Sacramento, Ray Kaiser Eames studied under the painter Hans Hofmann in New York, before moving on to the Cranbrook Academy. It was here that she met Charles Eames and helped him and Eero Saarinen in the preparations for their designs for the Museum of Modern Art's 'Organic Design in Home Furnishings' (1940). Eames and Saarinen's designs, produced by moulding plywood into intricate curves, won them first prize.

Charles and Ray Eames married in 1941 and relocated to California, where they carried on designing and developing furniture using moulded plywood. In 1946 Evans Products started to manufacture their furniture. The influential architectural critic of the time, Esther McCoy, proclaimed their moulded plywood chair to be 'the chair of the century'. In addition to their moulded plywood products, Charles and Ray Eames designed and built their own house in Pacific Palisades, California. In terms of design, Pacific Palisades is widely thought to be one of the major post-war residences built anywhere in the world. Renowned for its design and innovative use of materials, the Eames' house has become an important destination to visit and learn for architects and designers from all over the globe.

Widely acknowledged as leading lights in the experimentation and exploration of materials and their application in design, by the late 1950s and early 1960s, Charles and Ray Eames were regularly working with several large clients including Herman Miller, Vitra and IBM. By the late 1950s, the couple had shifted their focus from plywood to other materials such as fibreglass, plastic, aluminium and leather. Among the pieces produced during this time was the Armchair Rod chair – the first to use a seat moulded from fibreglass-reinforced plastic. Attaching the seat shell to different bases, such as a steel-rod frame or rockers, made the chair more versatile. The Eames' iconic Lounge chair and foot stool, also designed during this period, became a status symbol of the 1970s.

Eero Saarinen

Eero Saarinen's architecture and design career was tragically cut short in 1961 at the relatively young age of 51. Nevertheless, he enjoyed a highly productive working life that spanned more than 20 years and, during this time, was responsible for some of the seminal furniture and building designs of the twentieth century.

Born 1910, Kirkkonummi, Finland
Importance Prolific creator of varied modernist designs
Died 1961, Ann Arbor, Michigan, United States

Saarinen's father was the celebrated Finnish architect, Eliel Saarinen – the first president of the Cranbrook Academy of Art. Born in Helsinki, Eero emigrated with his family to the United States in 1923. He initially studied sculpture at the Académie de la Grande Chaumière in Paris from 1929 to 1930 before going on to study architecture at Yale University in New Haven, Connecticut. He graduated in 1934.

Saarinen received a scholarship from Yale that enabled him to travel to Europe for a year in 1934 to 1935. On his return, he taught at the Cranbrook Academy of Art, and in 1937, he began collaborating with Charles Eames, a fellow staff member at Cranbrook. The collaboration with Eames resulted in a number of innovative, prize-winning furniture designs for the Museum of Modern Art's 'Organic Design in Home Furnishings' competition (1940). Their competition submissions included a modular storage system and a series of chairs with single-form compound-moulded plywood seat shells. Their chairs were among the most significant designs of the twentieth century, and signalled a new direction in furniture design. They also led to Saarinen producing several highly successful furniture designs for Knoll International, including the No 70 Womb chair (1947 to 1948).

Much of Saarinen's furniture design was aimed at alleviating the visual clutter found beneath the seat and tables of a lot of 1950s furniture – in his words, an attempt to 'clean up the slum of legs' in domestic interiors. Early attempts, such as his Grasshopper Model No 61 (1946 to 1947) were deemed 'nice', by Florence Knoll, but were not great commercial successes. Critical success did arrive, however, with his Tulip Group of tables and chairs. The organic aesthetic of the Model No 150 Tulip chair (1955 to 1956) adheres to much of the early 1960s moulded concrete architecture and plastic futuristic designs. Although the Tulip chair appears to be made from a single unified whole, the pedestal is actually made from aluminium while the seat is made from fibreglass shell. It was only the limitations of plastics technology at the time that prevented Saarinen of achieving his objective of a single-material, single-form chair.

Saarinen was involved in the design of more than 60 buildings during his rather short architectural career. Several of them are counted among the most powerful American iconic landmarks, and include his much-praised masterpiece, the TWA Terminal at New York's John F Kennedy Airport (1956 to 1962). An innovator in the field, Saarinen made bold use of new materials and technologies such as reinforced concrete and curtain-wall technology. His building designs vary greatly in style, displaying influences from the cubic-style work of Mies van der Rohe to the organic, flowing shapes achieved in concrete by Le Corbusier at the Ronchamp chapel. He posthumously received the Gold Medal from the American Institute of Architects in 1961.

Verner Panton

Verner Panton was not the quintessential Scandinavian designer. He was more influenced by European and American design, particularly the designs that ventured into the op art and futuristic narratives that were being explored by the likes of Joe Colombo and Archizoom during the 1960s and 1970s.

Born 1926, Gamtofte, Denmark
Importance Created the first injection-moulded chair
Died 1998, Copenhagen, Denmark

Panton trained at Odense Technical School, initially as an architectural engineer, before studying architecture at the Royal Academy of the Arts in Copenhagen. After leaving the Academy, in 1950, he spent two years working with Arne Jacobsen, the renowned Danish architect and designer.

In 1955, Panton established his own design practice and received recognition for his innovative architectural proposals including the Cardboard House and the Plastic House. In 1958, he received the first of his major commissions, which involved a rebuild and extension of the Komigen Inn (Come Again Inn) on the Danish island of Funen. The revolutionary design proposal included an all-red interior that housed his famous Cone chair (1958). The Cone chair, and its younger sibling the Heart chair (1959), went into mass production by Plus-Linje in 1959 and instantly became iconic symbols of Panton's style. Both chairs embody the wide-ranging visual language of Panton's designs, using cladding and cushions to provide vibrant colours, and which adhere to his revolutionary shapes and forms.

Panton is, undoubtedly, most famous for his iconic, revolutionary stacking side chair, also known as the 'S chair' or the 'his chair'. It was developed over a period of 12 years starting from a bent-plywood S chair model 275 for Thonet GmbH (1955), through many sketched iterations completed in 1962, to the first production versions in fibreglass-reinforced polyester (1967). In 1963, Vitra, the licensed producers of the Herman Miller range, began work on Panton's design. Herman Miller were initially reluctant to produce the chair claiming: 'It is at most a sculpture, but not a chair'. In 1967, after much experimentation, the first trial series of 100 to 150 chairs were released. More refinements were made to the chair before the final version went into mass production in 1968.

The S chair marked a significant event in industrial furniture production in that it was the first chair cast all in one piece and made entirely from synthetic material. Panton pushed the limits of polyurethane – a relatively new material at the time – by creating a piece of furniture that required no assembly or hand finishing.

Although the S chair is Panton's defining product, his influence is far further reaching. He explored furniture and interior spaces by constantly engaging with new materials and production techniques and by remaining true to his own interest in colour, pattern and form. Widely regarded as taking a revolutionary rather than evolutionary approach to design, Verner Panton continued to produce highly innovative, bold and playful designs using state-of-the-art technology well into the 1980s.

PLASTICS

Man-made materials featured significantly in twentieth-century design. The development and application of plastics, and their effect on mass consumerism, has been so profound that commentators refer to the period as the 'plastics age'.

Plastic is generally thought of as a twentieth-century invention, but there have always been natural plastics such as shellac, casein, amber and tortoiseshell, all of which have long been used in the manufacture of goods. During the 1840s Alexander Parkes, an English chemist and inventor, developed the first synthetic material, cellulose nitrate, which he exhibited as Parkesine, the world's first plastic, in 1862. It was immediately applied in the manufacture of decorative objects, cutlery handles and various other products including gentlemen's collars and cuffs. In 1869, the American, John Wesley Hyatt, patented a process for the manufacture of a nitrate cellulose composition he named Celluloid.

Leo Baekeland, a Belgian-born chemist, discovered Bakelite in 1907, which was used in a number of applications for the emerging telecommunications industry at the time. Two decades later, it was championed by designers of the art deco period, who embraced its range of bright colours and durability in making all manner of domestic wares from ashtrays to napkin rings. Its peak during the Depression years also owes much to its application for cheap and cheerful costume jewellery at a time when money was scarce.

In the early 1920s, Hermann Staudinger, a German chemist, made a remarkable discovery that would alter the nature of the plastics industry forever. He found that plastics were made from long chains of thousands of molecules linked together. The development of these 'super polymers' supported the invention of many other new products over the course of the next few decades. By the late 1920s the development of polyvinyl chloride (PVC) continued apace with its first use as an insulator for electric cables. Today, PVC is available in two forms – rigid or flexible – with the latter being used extensively in the packaging industry.

By the end of the Second World War, plastics included polyethylene (PE), polystyrene (PS), Perspex, polyurethane (PU), polypropylene (PP), acrylonitrile-butadiene-styrene (ABS) and polyethylene terephthalate (PET), many of which are still in wide use today. Around 1952, the Italian Giulio Natta with Karl Ziegler invented polypropylene – an achievement that earned them the Nobel Prize for chemistry. Joe Colombo was one of the chief exponents of experimenting with the latest production processes and newly developed plastics including fibreglass, ABS, PVC and polyethylene.

The 1960s was a rich period for product design. The decade saw the introduction of a range of innovative new materials, including soft and hard foams with a protective skin, wet-look polyurethane and transparent acrylic. Plastics played a massive role in the 'space race' of the 1960s, with their lightweight and versatile nature making it a perfect material for several applications. The 1970s saw the advent of several new 'super polymers', developed in an effort to replace some metals.

Today, no modern industry would be able to function without plastic. The huge rise in global telecommunications has been made possible by developments in plastics technology. Moreover, there are a multitude of products that rely on plastics of one sort or another from computers to furniture, which all use the strength and flexibility of this amazing material.

Joe Colombo

Cesare 'Joe' Colombo was a prolific and illustrious Italian designer intent on creating state-of-the-art product, interior and furniture designs. A creative visionary, he was obsessed with new materials, processes and technologies and how they could be exploited to change human interactions and living.

Born 1930, Milan, Italy
Importance Designed the world's first single-component chair
Died 1971, Milan, Italy

Colombo, who died at the young age of 41, was a designer for a relatively short period of time. He studied painting and, later, architecture at the Academy of Fine Arts of Brera, Milan (1949) and at the Milan Polytechnic (1954). Following his father's death, Colombo and his brother Gianni took over the running of the family business. The company, which manufactured electrical equipment, allowed Colombo to explore new processes and materials, which further engaged his interest in product

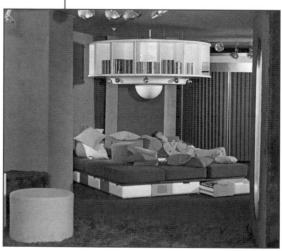

design. In 1962, with his brother Gianni, Colombo developed the Acrilica desk lamp for O-Luce. Later that year, he opened his own design practice in Milan, initially focusing on architectural and interior design projects. He designed many products and interiors for a long list of clients, including

Kartell, Alessi, Alitalia, Bieffeplast, Flexform and Boffi. Using his knowledge and experience of plastics and processes, he designed the first adult-sized chair to be manufactured in injection-moulded plastic (ABS) when he created the Universale No 4860 chair for Kartell between 1965 and 1967. In keeping with his desire to create machines for living, one of his most forward-looking ideas was his integrated microenvironment, the Visiona 1 habitat of the future shown at Bayer's Visiona exhibition in 1969 – a space age interior where furnishings transmuted into structural elements and vice versa. Colombo's uniquely forward-thinking approach to producing new concepts for furniture and interiors meant that he often completely redefined what an object was and how it might be used.

This multi-functionality and adaptability was a common theme in Colombo's work. The Boby trolley (1968), for example, was created from interchangeable parts, which allowed for owner configuration, and quickly became an iconic and popular product used by designers, hairdressers and other discerning consumers. Colombo's aim of producing multi-functional, universal, adaptable products extended to his Additional Living System (1967 to 1968), his Tube chair (1969 to 1970) and his Multi chair (1970).

Colombo received Associazione per il Disegno Industriale awards in 1967 and 1968 as well as a Premio Compasso d'Oro (see page 33) in 1970. In a final act, as it ultimately became, Colombo created his Total Furnishing Unit (1971) which was a highly influential example of 'Uniblock' design, housing everything from kitchen and bathroom facilities to sleeping and storage space and entertainment and study facilities. The resultant solution presented the ultimate machine for living – an all-encompassing facility servicing all human requirements. Tragically, Colombo died of a heart attack in 1971 and never saw his vision unveiled at the 'Italy: The New Domestic Landscape' exhibition at the Museum of Modern Art (MoMA), New York in 1972.

INJECTION-MOULDED PLASTIC [ABS]
Injection moulding produces high numbers of plastic products of high quality very quickly. Plastic granules are melted and injected, under pressure, into a mould. After cooling the mould is opened up and the product released.

Ron Arad

Avant-garde designer Ron Arad is considered one of the key figures of contemporary architecture and design. A graduate of the Architectural Association in London, he has studiously sought to avoid categorisation by either curators or critics. Although he never wanted a profession as such – be it as an architect, a product designer or furniture designer – his reputation in each of these fields is formidable as he continues to question established design practices.

Born 1951, Tel Aviv, Israel
Importance Rejected orthodoxy and pioneered 'one-off' designs over mass production

Arad studied at the Bezalel Academy of Art and Design in Jerusalem before moving to London in 1973. It was here, at the Architectural Association, and studying under two of the greatest architectural theorists, Peter Cook and Bernard Tschumi, that he developed his own unique approach to architecture and design. After graduating in 1979, he set up his own company, One Off, with Caroline Thorman (1981), followed by a showroom in Covent Garden a couple years later. In 1989, Ron Arad Associates began operating out of their current studio in Chalk Farm, north London.

The Architectural Association in London has a reputation for encouraging the avant-garde and a history of producing innovative designers and thinkers rather than practising architects, and Arad is no exception. His well-documented opposition to orthodoxy is evident in the way he set out, during the early years of his career, to challenge the principles of mass production in the furniture design industry by designing a number of 'one-off' designs. Describing himself as an outsider, Arad has regularly stated that he has '…an aversion to conventions. I prefer truth to sincerity. Dylan says in one of his songs – to live outside the law you have to be honest'. Among his early pieces are the Rover chair (1981, a *Rover 200* car seat mounted on a frame of builders' scaffolding), a stereo cast in concrete (1983), and a beaten-steel Tinker chair (1988).

His later furniture designs of the mid-1980s, such as the Big Easy Series (1988 to 1989), are less rough and ready than his earlier work. Indeed much of his steel designs of the late 1980s are highly labour intensive and costly to manufacture. During this period, Arad consciously distanced himself from mass-production techniques, preferring to concentrate on what has been termed 'art furniture'. Arad is arguably now better known for his furniture design than his architectural projects (which include commissions to design interiors for Belgo restaurants, London (1994 and 1995), and an entire floor of Selfridges department store on London's Oxford Street (2001). His largest built project, to date, is the 1994 Tel Aviv Opera House.

As well as his one-off designs, Arad also produces pieces for mass production, and has an impressive list of clients, including Driade, Cassina, Alessi, Vitra and Magis. He has exhibited at major museums and galleries throughout the world and his work can be seen in many public collections.

Superstar Talent
Marc Newson

Bursting onto the international design scene in the early 1990s, Marc Newson was almost immediately heralded as a superstar talent. He is widely regarded as one of the most successful and prominent designers of his era and many critics have compared his significance to that of Philippe Starck in the 1980s.

Born 1963, Sydney, Australia
Importance One of the most successful designers of the new millennium

With work exhibited everywhere from the Museum of Modern Art (MoMA) in New York and the Design Museum, London, to the Musée des Arts Décoratifs in Paris, Newson has convincingly established himself as one of the most important designers of his generation. He appears to be able to turn his hand to the most demanding of creative briefs, having undertaken a wide range of projects from chairs to concept cars and a host of interiors for clients across the globe. In this context, he can claim to be a truly multidisciplinary designer. Much of his work is strongly influenced by biomorphism and the streamlined forms prevalent in 1950s America.

Newson grew up in Australia, travelling to Europe and Asia as a

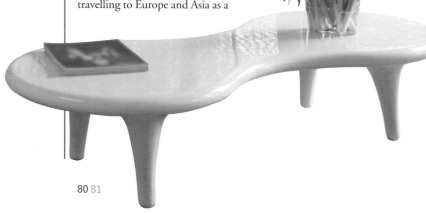

child. His mother worked in an architect's office and he has claimed that his upbringing in Sydney was peppered with exposure to classic pieces of design from the likes of Le Corbusier, Joe Colombo and Enzo Mari. He studied jewellery design and sculpture having initially enrolled to do a fine art course at the Sydney College of Arts. Two years after graduating, in 1984, he founded the POD design studio where he started experimenting with furniture design.

After receiving a $10,000 grant from the Australian Crafts Council, Newson staged an exhibition at Sydney's most prestigious art space, the Roslyn Oxley Gallery (1986). Applying the skills he had learned in jewellery design, in combination with some do-it-yourself adaptations of industrial processes, he began sculpting forms and bashing metal together. The five pieces he created for the Roslyn Oxley Gallery included his Cone chair (1986), his Boat chair (1986) and his masterpiece, the iconic Lockheed Lounge chair (1986) – the most expensive piece of furniture by a living designer ever to sell at auction – and which started out as a piece of foam that Newson sculpted over the course of a few days.

A chance encounter with Tentuo Kurosaki in Tokyo, 1987, led to Newson working with his company, Idée, from around 1988. It was during this time that Newson was able to put some of his own designs into production including the Embryo chair (1988), the Super Guppy lamp (1987), the Black Hole table (1988) and the Felt chair (1989), all of which were widely exhibited in Asia and Europe.

By the early 1990s, Newson had firmly established his reputation as an internationally acclaimed designer, winning commissions from prestigious European manufacturers such as Flos for lighting, Cappellini and Moroso for furniture, and Alessi for a range of domestic products. He has won a number of major design awards and in 2006, he was appointed a Royal Designer for Industry.

Josiah Wedgwood

One of several Staffordshire potters of his era, Josiah Wedgwood stood out above the rest both as a businessman and an innovator. His approach to manufacturing involved splitting the labour in order to create a production line, in which design was separate from manufacture and production. Furthermore, he demonstrated both an astute identification of consumer needs and an ability to design good products to satisfy those needs.

Born 1730, Stoke-on-Trent, England
Importance First manufacturer to introduce the concept of division of labour
Died 1795, Stoke-on-Trent, England

Wedgwood spent much of his early life in the Wedgwood family pottery business, starting out as a pottery 'thrower' in 1739, following the death of his father. After working with his brother, Thomas, for 20 years, he opened his own pottery works at Ivy House in 1759, subsequently moving to the Brick House Works in 1763, before building the factory, Etruria, for which he is best known. Among his concerns here, was the fair treatment of his employees – so much so, that he built a village beside the factory so that they could experience a good quality of life.

Social changes, including the increased popularity of the custom of tea and coffee drinking, plus the increased consumption of hot cooked meals among the English population, led to increased demand for pottery. Wedgwood responded quickest to these social changes and recognised the potential for the creation of a pottery industry within his local community.

Using designs by artists such as John Flaxman, he produced earthenware that was both affordable and aesthetically pleasing. Among his ceramics was a durable, cream-coloured earthenware, which became known as Queen's ware following his appointment to Queen Charlotte in 1762.

Wedgwood was responsible for revolutionising pottery manufacturing techniques, in order to increase production and sell to a wider market in an era that was largely characterised by production principally involving making by hand. With the dawn of the industrial age came mechanisation, which largely supplanted the handmade and replaced the human with the machine. The potter's wheel, central to the production of handmade pottery pieces prior to 1730, was replaced by the use of moulds – an innovation that led to new categories of pottery workers, as it divided up the labour that was once carried out by a single hand-throwing potter. Job titles such as mould carvers and mould designers became commonplace, while the change dispensed with the need for highly skilled master potters who were replaced by lesser-experienced teams of men and boys. The more the labour was divided, the quicker the process became, producing units at an increased rate. Faster production led to wider availability and increased affordability. Embracing these principles, Wedgwood undoubtedly transformed the pottery industry.

Wedgwood was also responsible for discovering new methods in glazing, including the matt, usually green or blue, Jasper ware and the black basalt ware. The royal seal of approval increased the attractiveness and saleability of his pottery, and he adopted clever and sophisticated marketing techniques, exploiting this connection to sell 'taste' to a swelling middle-class market.

William Morris

William Morris was, among many things, an author, a poet and dreamer, a businessman and a political campaigner, but he is probably best known as the most significant figure in the arts and crafts movement. He was one of the most influential voices in Victorian art, design and architecture, and his influence spread far into the twentieth century, as an advocate for the renewal of artistic handwork.

Born 1834, London, England
Importance Founding member of the arts and crafts movement in Britain
Died 1896, London, England

Morris studied theology at Exeter College, Oxford, before training briefly as an architect at the office of the eminent Gothic Revivalist George Edmund Street. He was hugely influenced by the social and artistic reformer, John Ruskin, and by the romantic escapism of the Pre-Raphaelite painters, which he viewed as 'the dawn of a new era of art'. For a brief period, he studied painting under the guidance of Dante Gabriel Rossetti, but quickly abandoned this in favour of working in the decorative arts.

Morris's first project was his own house, the Red House in Bexleyheath, Kent, which had been designed in 1859 by the architect Philip Webb. Morris furnished his house with murals, stained glass and furniture aided by his close circle of friends. Around this time, Morris and his friends conceived the idea of 'The Firm' (1861), which later became Morris, Marshall, Faulkner and Company, and had Rossetti, Webb, Edward Burne-Jones and Ford Madox Brown among its members. Morris disseminated both his design work and his social reformist theories through his own publications, which were printed by his own Kelmscott Press, founded in 1890. Today, the Kelmscott books are respected widely for the innovative and creative type designs, page borders and bindings.

Morris's company aimed to put its social-reform theories into action by designing a wide range of items including furniture, stained glass, wallpaper, ceramics, carpets and textiles, all promoting the virtues of simplicity, utility and beauty. Morris was a committed socialist, who wished to bring good design to the masses, but he refused to accept the increasing mechanisation and mass production of the period. He saw the effects of industrialisation and mass production as environmentally polluting, producing poor-quality wares and as a 'devilish capitalistic

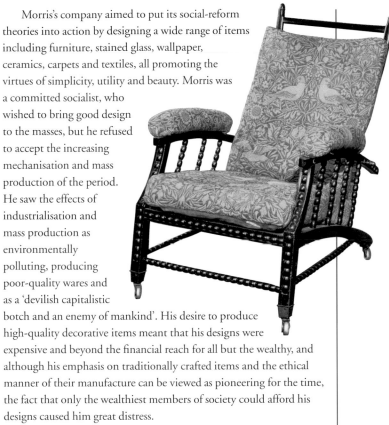

botch and an enemy of mankind'. His desire to produce high-quality decorative items meant that his designs were expensive and beyond the financial reach for all but the wealthy, and although his emphasis on traditionally crafted items and the ethical manner of their manufacture can be viewed as pioneering for the time, the fact that only the wealthiest members of society could afford his designs caused him great distress.

Today, Morris's opinions on the value of utility, simplicity and concern for the environment continue to resonate with many. Moreover, his views on the importance of producing high-quality, morally appropriate objects, and the use of design as a democratic tool for social reform, has had an enormous impact on many designers and design movements throughout the twentieth century.

Joseph Hoffmann

An important figure in the Vienna Secession, Joseph Hoffmann trained at the Vienna Academy of Arts, under the leading architect Otto Wagner. He went on to become one of the most important architects and designers in Europe at the start of the twentieth century. Ultimately his style and methods would inform the development of the modernist movement.

Born 1870, Pirnitz, Moravia (now Czech Republic)
Importance Abstract architect and product designer; forerunner of the modernist movement
Died 1956, Vienna, Austria

Hoffmann was at the heart of Viennese creativity at the turn of the twentieth century and is recognised as the leader of Viennese architecture. He worked in the International Style, finding himself influenced by luminaries such as the Glasgow Four and, in particular, the styling of Charles Rennie Mackintosh.

Hoffman started his career as an architect and continued to run his own successful practice throughout his life. His 'Purkersdorf Sanatorium' (1903 to 1906) and the 'Palais Stoclet', Brussels (1905 to 1911) epitomised his use of limited adornment, simple geometric language, refined window forms and flat roofs. During his time as an employee of Otto Wagner, Hoffmann co-founded the Vienna Secession in 1897. 'Die Sezession', as it became known, was a platform for artistic creativity and exhibition in defiance of the existing Vienna Künstlerhaus and it's historicist methods. Among his co-founders were Gustav Klimt, Joseph Maria Olbrich, Otto Wagner and Koloman Moser. The main result was the purpose-built Secession Building (1897) by Joseph Marie Olbrich.

In 1903 Hoffmann and Koloman Moser instigated the foundation of the Wiener Werkstätte, an environment in which designers worked as part of a collaborative organisation. The philosophy of the Werkstätte was heavily influenced by Hoffmann and Moser's previous

travels to Britain where they had encountered the arts and crafts movement. This environment offered Hoffmann a greater scope to explore his creativity in terms of design. He is well-known for his home wares, metalwork, architecture, and furniture designs of this period, many of which were executed by members of the Wiener Werkstätte. Alongside exquisite silverware are examples of glassware for Loetz Witwe glassworks and the majestic Sitting Machine chair (circa 1905). The same decorative motifs are evident throughout his work, particularly the application of simple geometric forms.

Following a difference of artistic opinion, in 1905, Klimt and Hoffmann left the Vienna Secession and together formed the Kunstschau (Arts Show). Hoffmann continued to work in both architecture and design and in 1910 produced his iconic Kubus chair. Hoffmann became revered for his pared down geometric approach, which when discussed in relation to its influence on modernism is simply referred to as 'Hoffmann's elegance'.

Further ventures in developing creative opportunities saw Hoffman act as a founding member of the Austrian Werkbund in 1912, which consisted of artists, architects, industrialists and designers. The Werkbund was to become influential in terms of architectural and industrial design within the modernist movement, and developed connections with the Bauhaus school (see page 90).

Gió Ponti

A true Renaissance man for modern times, Gióvanni (Gió) Ponti was one of Italy's premier twentieth-century designers. He created furniture, metalwork and ceramics and was also a highly respected architect, teacher, and a prolific writer, critic and editor. His widely celebrated classic Superleggera chair for Cassina (1957) has become one of the best-known chair designs of all time.

Born 1891, Milan, Italy
Importance Highly influential Italian product designer, industrial designer and architect
Died 1979, Milan, Italy

Ponti graduated in 1921, with a degree in architecture from Milan Polytechnic and subsequently set up a studio with the architects Mino Fiocchi and Emilio Lancia.

From 1923 to 1930 he worked for the long-established Società Ceramica Richard-Ginori in Doccia, where he designed porcelain wares decorated with neoclassical motifs, some of which were awarded a Grand Prix at the 1925 Exposition Internationale des Arts Décoratifs et Industriels Modernes, in Paris. While there, he turned the company into a role model of industrial design excellence by decorating simple ceramic forms with elegant motifs. Ponti also designed low-cost furniture for the La Rinascente store in the 1920s, and was director of the Monza Biennale exhibitions between 1925 and 1979.

In 1928, Ponti founded the monthly Italian design magazine *Domus*, which he helped establish as Europe's most influential architecture and design magazine. He resigned as editor of *Domus*, in

'Industry is the style of the twentieth century, its mode of creation.'

1921, and set up the magazine *Stile*, which he edited until 1947. In 1948, however, he returned to *Domus*, and remained there as editor until his death in September 1979.

Ponti received a number of awards throughout his life, including the title of Commander of the Royal Vasa Order in Stockholm (1934), the art prize of the Accademia d'Italia, an honorary doctorate from the Royal College of Art in London, and a gold medal from the Académie d'Architecture in Paris.

He continued his prolific output in many different design fields during the 1940s producing sets and costumes for La Scala opera house (1947), creating multicoloured glass bottles, glasses and a chandelier for Venini (1946 to 1950), and he designed the famous La Pavoni coffee machine (1949) – a gleaming chrome, organic-dynamic sculpture of a coffee machine that became a trademark of the espresso bars of the 1950s. Going on to focus more on industrial design, Ponti produced the Superleggera ('superlight') chair in 1957. Based on the ubiquitous, age-old Italian rustic chair, it was designed to be strong, yet light enough that it could be lifted up using only one finger. His Distex armchair (1953) was also well-received.

During the late 1940s and throughout the 1950s, Ponti collaborated with Piero Fornasetti, renowned for his surreal, neoclassical style, on several furniture and interior-design projects including the Casino at San Remo (1950).

Although Ponti's chair designs rank among his most famous creations, he has designed many other objects for the home and for industry, including cutlery, sanitary ware and ovoid lighting fixtures.

THE BAUHAUS

The Bauhaus, which translates as 'building house', was established to bring unity to the disciplines of art and design. Walter Gropius, the school's first director, viewed construction as an important social and intellectual endeavour and this sentiment permeated much of the early teaching at the school. Although there have been other great schools in the history of design – notably the Cranbrook Academy of Art and The Chicago Institute of Design, both in the United States – none has matched the importance and impact achieved by the Bauhaus.

In 1919 the Grand Ducal Saxon School of Arts and Crafts in Weimar merged with the Weimar Academy of Fine Art, with architect Walter Gropius appointed director. He renamed the school 'Bauhaus' and appointed new staff including the artist Paul Klee and designer Oskar Schlemmer. Over time, the staff of the Bauhaus came to include many of the most important designers of the twentieth century, including Mies van der Rohe and László Moholy-Nagy (who went on to found the Chicago Institute of Design), as well as artists such as Josef Albers and Wassily Kandinsky. Other influential designers, including Marcel Breuer, Anni Albers, Marianne Brandt and Wilhelm Wagenfeld, started as students here before taking up teaching posts.

Many significant pieces of design work were created at the Bauhaus. These include Marcel Breuer's Wassily chair, which was revolutionary in its use of tubular steel, Wilhelm Wagenfeld's Bauhaus table lamp – a timeless classic – and Marianne Brandt's geometric metalware. Many pieces are produced under license today.

The school's heyday was probably the mid-1920s, with the creation of a new building for the school in Dessau and the appointment of leading pupils, such as Breuer and Bayer, as instructors. However, throughout its 14-year existence there were also many problems, not least internal conflict over the direction the school should take. Gropius clashed with Swiss artist Johannes Itten, whose views were at odds with his more rational approach to design.

After Itten's departure in December 1922, Gropius was free to take a more modern, constructivist approach. The 1923 student exhibition reflected this, featuring a number of important designs including Gerrit Rietveld's Red Blue Chair of 1918 to 1923 and graphics incorporating the New Typography inspired by De Stijl and Russian constructivism respectively. The school also became more egalitarian, freeing women from the pottery and textiles workshops they had previously been restricted to.

The Bauhaus moved to Dessau in 1925, after the Social-Democrat government that funded the Bauhaus in Weimar lost power to the Nazis. Gropius built a new building, based on highly rational, prefabricated structural elements, heralding a move away from the school's emphasis on craft, and towards industrial functionalism. Although the school enjoyed a number of successful years there, the rise of Nazism put pressure on the Bauhaus: it was seen as un-German, and in 1928 Gropius resigned. Despite the attempts of his successors, Hannes Meyer and Mies van der Rohe, to keep the school going, the Bauhaus was dissolved on 19 July 1933.

Many of the Bauhaus luminaries emigrated to the United States to escape persecution by the Nazis. Gropius became professor of architecture at Harvard in 1937, where Breuer also taught. In 1938, a retrospective of Bauhaus design was held at the Museum of Modern Art (MoMA), New York, which reinforced the school as the most important design institution of the twentieth century.

Marianne Brandt

During the early twentieth century, the majority of women connected with the Bauhaus (see page 90) made their names in traditional arts and crafts areas such as textiles, weaving and pottery. Brandt, however, established herself as a first-class designer of metalware, and several of her tea services and lamps have become classics. Alessi have produced her designs since the mid-1980s.

Born 1893, Chemnitz, Germany
Importance Pioneering female designer of metal home wares in the Bauhaus style
Died 1983, Kirchberg, Germany

Brandt studied painting and sculpture at the Grand-Ducal Saxon Academy of Fine Art from 1911 to 1918, and enrolled at the Bauhaus in Weimar in 1923, entering the male-dominated metal workshop directed by László Moholy-Nagy. She remained at the Bauhaus from 1924 to 1929 and studied under the likes of Josef Albers, Paul Klee and Wassily Kandinsky.

Becoming deputy director of the metal workshop in 1928, Brandt was responsible for setting up a number of industrial collaborations with the lighting manufacturers Körting and Mathieson AG (Kandem) in Leipzig and Schwinter and Graff in Berlin. She worked with fellow Bauhaus metalworkers, Christian Dell and Hans Przyrembel, and, in 1928, co-designed the 702 Kandem bedside lamp with Hin Briedendieck for Körting and Mathieson. Among the 70 or so designs Brandt produced during her years at the Bauhaus, her lamp designs were particularly well received because of their suitability for mass production. Several of them have gone on to become icons of

'I was never aware that my designs were revolutionary, I have simply followed my ideas and the need of the moment.'

Bauhaus design, as has her brass hemispherical teapot (1924). Her designs represent the archetypal philosophy of the Bauhaus metal workshop in their reduction to the purest geometric ideals in order to appear as if mass-produced. For example, the Table Clock (circa 1930), produced for the Ruppelwerk Metalware Factory in Gotha, epitomises her lucid formal language, which reduces household objects to elemental geometric forms.

Brandt left the Bauhaus in 1929. For a short time after that, she worked with Walter Gropius in his architectural firm in Berlin creating design solutions for mass-produced, modular furniture. Between 1930 and 1933, she held the position of head of design at the Ruppelwerk Metalware Factory. In 1949, she was invited to teach at Dresden's Hochschule der Bildenden Künste, and from 1951 to 1954 she taught at the Institut für Angewandte Kunst in Berlin-Weißensee.

It is Brandt's industrial-design work that is considered of the greatest significance today. Ironically, however, she never succeeded in attracting significant freelance work during her heyday, unlike many of her Bauhaus peers. She is best known for her iconic metalwork designs for the Bauhaus – the lamps and teapots, but also ashtrays and bowls – and her work is in the permanent collection of the Busch-Reisinger Museum at Harvard University, in the US. She also commands respect as one of the very first women to design for industrial mass production – a field that has historically been the sole domain of male designers.

Wilhelm Wagenfeld

Wilhelm Wagenfeld was one of the fathers of modern industrial design in Germany and a leading advocate of the ideals of 'good form'. Today, as a renowned designer of the Bauhaus school (see page 90), his functional and aesthetically restrained industrial designs are seen to exemplify the ambitions of that once-great design institution.

Born 1900, Bremen, Germany
Importance Highly influential Bauhaus industrial designer
Died 1990, Stuttgart, Germany

Wagenfeld was born in Bremen and served an apprenticeship in the drafting office of a silver factory, Silberwarenfabrik Koch and Bergfeld, before studying at the Drawing Academy in Hanau, in 1919. In 1923, he enrolled on the preliminary course at the Bauhaus in Weimar and studied under László Moholy-Nagy in the school's metal workshop. In collaboration with Karl J Jucker, he designed the, now famous, Bauhaus table lamp (1923 to 1924), which was put into production by the workshop.

After leaving the Bauhaus, in 1929, Wagenfeld became a professor at the Staatliche Kunsthochschule Berlin from 1931 to 1935 but gave up teaching when he was appointed artistic director of the Lausitz Glassworks, working on a number of projects employing industrial mass-production techniques. Perhaps the most successful of the projects developed in his time at the glassworks were his Kubus range (1938) of modular, stacking storage containers for kitchen use. He also designed many other glass products that were appropriate for industrial mass production, including utilitarian pressed-glass ranges of wine and beer glasses, bottles and jars.

Among his other well-known pieces are a heat-resistant glass tea set for Schott & Gen Glassworks in Jena (1930 to 1934) and Max und Moritz salt and pepper shakers for WMF (1952 to 1953). His later projects include in-flight meal trays for Lufthansa (1955), porcelain tableware for Rosenthal (1938), appliances for Braun and lighting for WMF and Schott.

Unlike the majority of Bauhaus teachers, who fled the country, Wagenfeld decided to remain in Germany at the outbreak of the Second World War and was deported to a Russian prisoner-of-war camp on the Eastern front because he refused to assist the Nazi regime. After the war, he articulated his functionalist approach to design in several journals including *Die Form* between 1947 and 1949. He also went on to establish his own design office in Stuttgart, in 1954, where he continued to develop his innovative approach to design. Today, he is seen as an important Bauhaus figure for the restrained nature of his designs. Many of his clear, functional pieces are now considered design classics of timeless beauty and continue to be widely bought and admired today for their functionality and their contribution to post-war German culture.

Wagenfeld received the Grand Prix at the Milan Triennial in 1957 and the Bundespreis Gute Form in 1969 and 1982. Bremen has honoured him with a museum (Wilhelm Wagenfeld Haus), and his works are collected by many of the most important museums throughout the world including the Museum of Modern Art (MoMA) in New York.

Home Wares

Achille Castiglioni

A major figure of twentieth-century Italian design, Achille Castiglioni worked with some of the most important product, furniture and lighting companies of recent times. He accumulated many awards during his career, including the Compasso d'Oro on eight occasions for independent pieces and a further one for recognition of his lifetime's work.

Born 1918, Milan, Italy
Importance
Incorporated existing objects in new industrial designs
Died 2002, Milan, Italy

Castiglioni was the figurehead of the design triumvirate that included his brothers as partners (Pier Giacomo and Livio), and with whom he designed many of his most iconic pieces. Following in the footsteps of Pier Giacomo, Castiglioni had joined his elder brother Livio's architectural practice in 1944. Livio left the partnership in 1952, but Achille and Pier Giacomo continued to work together until the latter's death, in 1968. The brothers worked in a manner that explored the use of objects in new and alternative forms, introducing ready-made parts in new and challenging ways. Endearing symbols of their design approach are evident in their famous Mezzadro stool (1957), which incorporated a traditional tractor seat, and the Sgabello per Telefono stool (1957), featuring a bicycle seat.

The Mezzadro stool's tractor seat was elevated to sitting height by use of a chromed, flat, bent-steel bar. Finished at the base with a wooden section, the seat acted as an anchor and point of balance. The simplicity of the form, and yet its attention to detail, offer a sublimely elegant and playful means of reinterpreting a seat that had previously been no more than a working tool. The Sgabello per Telefono or 'Stella' stool, as it is commonly known, further plays with alternative possibilities for ready-made objects. The form is that of a bicycle saddle atop a pink steel tube that is, in turn, connected to a perfectly

balanced domed base. The instability of the stool dictates its terms of use and explains Castiglioni's exact thinking in his attempt to create a piece of furniture that he could perch upon and move about on while using the phone. Such playful experimentation became a trademark of Castiglioni's work, and yet the brothers developed many other, elegant and completely original, designed objects as well, from radios to writing desks. The Arco floor lamp (1962) is a prime example of the elegant refinement that particularly defines Achille's work: emerging from a solid marble base, a telescopic steel stem rises in an immense, sweeping arc, to suspend the light over a dining table, seemingly floating in air.

Following the death of Pier Giacomo, Achille continued to work on his own and produced yet more iconic products, lights and furniture. Working with companies such as Flos, Zanotta and Alessi, he continued to produce award-winning work that included the Frisbi pendant light (1978), the AC08 – Grand Prix cutlery set (1997) and the 712 Joy shelving unit (1989). As well as being a creative force and inspirational stylist, he was significantly involved with the championing of design and, with his brothers, was a significant contributor to the founding of the Industrial Design Association and the subsequent Compasso d'Oro awards (see page 31). Castiglioni was also involved in the development of the Milan Triennial (see page 21), and participated in every event from its inception through to his death in 2002. He was similarly active as a design professor, working for 10 years at the Turin Polytechnic followed by a further five years at the Milan Polytechnic.

Terence Conran

Terence Conran first came to prominence in the 1960s, while advocating the merits of good design for the British general public. A leading designer in many fields and with multiple successes in the fields of publishing, architecture and the restaurant business, his flair for creative retailing became apparent when he opened his first Habitat store on London's Fulham Road in 1964. Arguably, Conran has done more to raise design awareness in Britain than any other individual.

Born 1931, Esher, England
Importance Pioneering designer of affordable, mass-market goods

Originally trained as a textile designer, Conran worked for the Rayon Centre, London, and subsequently as an interior designer for Dennis Lennon between 1951 and 1952. During the 1950s he built up his business as a freelance designer, founding the Conran Design Group in 1956 with John Stephenson.

Habitat sold Conran's furniture as well as French farmhouse kitchenware, pale wood tables and ethnic rugs. The shop was an immediate success and, by 1973, there were 18 branches throughout the United Kingdom. Later the store expanded to France, the United States, and now also operates under license in countries such as Iceland, Japan and Singapore. Conran's retail empire expanded significantly in the 1980s, first in a merger with the children's store, Mothercare, in 1982, and in a takeover of Heal's prestigious furniture firm in 1983. His Storehouse Group owned over 1,000 outlets by 1990 selling affordable, well-designed goods.

During the 1980s, Conran formed a joint publishing venture with Octopus Books and Conran/Octopus have since published books on interior design, cookery and gardening – all reflecting Conran's personal beliefs on style and design. As architectural designers,

Conran's company can be credited with two RIBA award-winning buildings in London (for extending the Michelin building, Fulham, and the Design Museum at Butler's Wharf). Founded in 1991, as Conran Restaurants, D&D London is one of Britain's most dynamic and successful restaurant groups. There are currently over 20 restaurants established in London, Paris and New York, many of which reflect Conran's reputation for creating contemporary interiors in historically important buildings.

'...if reasonable and intelligent people are offered something that is well made, well designed, of a decent quality and at a price they can afford, then they will like and buy it.'

In 1980, Conran established the Conran Foundation, a charitable fund dedicated to educating the public and British industry on the values of 'good design', which funded the Boilerhouse Project at the Victoria and Albert Museum from 1982 to 1986. In 1989, almost three years after the Boilerhouse Project closed, the Design Museum opened in Butler's Wharf, on the south bank of the Thames – the first museum in the world to be dedicated to the promotion and examination of design. Conran is currently the Provost of the Royal College of Art in London and was awarded The Prince Philip Designer of the Year award in 2004 for his services to design. He was knighted in 1983.

Home Wares

CORPORATE IDENTITY

Every single day of our lives is dominated by a plethora of branded goods and brand names. From breakfast cereals to newspapers, sportscars to aftershave, wristwatches to football clubs – each brand that we embrace says something about us as consumers. We regularly call products and services by their brands such as 'my new Volkswagen' or ' my old Levi's'. The brand is at the very core of our society. The success or failure of many companies and organisations all over the world is heavily dependant on the strength of their brand. Every business wants to be a customer's first choice and building a successful brand can play a significant part in making that happen.

Branding is the process of attaching a name and, therefore, a reputation to something or someone. The origin of the term 'brand' derives from the practice of literally marking or stamping property – sometimes with a hot iron – just as cattle or sheep would be marked as belonging to a particular farm or herd. The most obvious feature of a brand is a name, logo, symbol or trademark that signals a product's origin. In almost every case, however, the brand itself has much greater significance than this.

A successful brand is based firmly on a company's core values, and extends to every conceivable interaction between its customer base and its suppliers. Customers often develop strong emotional attachments to specific brands, which can facilitate long-lasting relationships between certain products and end-users. Strong brands, therefore, can contribute significantly to a company's overall commercial success.

Many customers consciously (sometimes, even, subconsciously) select one product or service over another, simply based on the strength of their respective brand values. So, in many ways, the brand is the key element when it comes to selling. Take, for example, the following well-known companies: Great Britain's Co-operative Group has the brand values of 'openness', 'honesty' and 'trust', all of which are seen as major assets to customers of its banking, insurance, food, travel, pharmacy and funeral businesses. The soft drinks company, Coca-Cola, arguably the most ubiquitous brand in the world, has been successfully promoting its brand values of 'fun', 'hip' and 'free spirit' for over 100 years. Finally, Puma's core brand values are the distinctly human qualities of 'spontaneity', 'authenticity' and 'individualism' – all characteristics that reinforce the brand as a major name in sports equipment.

A company's corporate identity is the uniform image of that company or an organisation, and is aimed at clearly distinguishing that company from its competitors and at making it instantly recognisable to consumers. Corporate identity allows customers, suppliers and staff to recognise, understand and clearly describe the organisation concerned.

The corporate identity of any company involves a multitude of elements that are both tangible and intangible. For example, tangible factors include the look and feel of printed and other material (text, colour), a company's products and services and promotional material such as advertising, marketing and company literature. Intangible factors include a company's values and the attitude of its employees. Corporate identity may even dictate the design of uniform clothing for its workers and social and behavioural norms towards its customers.

Michael Graves

An American architect and designer of great significance, Michael Graves is credited with being one of the world's first postmodernists. Highly influenced in his early career by the sleek, white cubic buildings of the likes of Le Corbusier and Joseff Hoffmann, he has gone on to receive international attention for his iconic designs.

Born 1934, Indianapolis, Indiana, United States
Importance Leading American architect and domestic goods' designer of the postmodern era

Graves set up his own architectural practice in 1964 and, five years later, came to prominence when he was featured as one of a group of five architects involved in an exhibition at the Museum of Modern Art (MoMA) in New York, which also included Peter Eisenman, Richard Meier, Charles Gwathmey and John Hejduk. Known as the 'New York Five', they greatly admired the classic early modern white, flat-roofed buildings such as Josef Hoffmann's Palais Stoclet.

Soon after the exhibition however, Graves exhibited signs of breaking away from his modernist tendencies and began to develop a style of his own, which manifested itself spectacularly when he built the complex and colourful Snyderman House in Fort Wayne, Indiana (1972). He continued to pursue his own unique style in architectural design with projects such as the Fargo-Moorhead Cultural Centre (1977 to 1978), which was an odd folly that featured a decorated bridge, plenty of visual references to the likes of the eighteenth-century French architect Claude-Nicolas Ledoux, classical Roman architecture and the bold, geometric shapes and colours of the art deco movement.

It was during the 1980s that Graves began to apply this same, postmodern, design approach to domestic products. He received international attention as a member of the hugely influential Memphis design group (see page 30) for his whimsical furniture designs such as the Hollywood-inspired Plaza dressing table (1981). He has also received critical acclaim for his product design work during this period, which included jewellery, ceramics and a number of domestic products for Alessi. By 1980, Graves was spending half of his time on the design of products and, became widely admired for the design of expensive, aesthetically charged, tableware, interiors, furniture and kitchen products. His iconic Whistling Bird Kettle, in particular, has been hugely successful, becoming one of the most popular designer objects of the postmodern period. It connected well with the demands and wishes of an increasingly fashion-conscious body of consumers in the 1980s. It is reported that Graves demanded a fee of $75,000 from the manufacturer for this design, but this has been more than repaid in the estimated sales of over two million units at approximately $125 each since its creation.

In 1999 Graves began designing everyday domestic products for the American retail group, Target. The goal of this collaboration was to bring good design to the American masses and it has been widely reported a huge success by both critics and consumers alike. Over the course of the last decade, Graves has created over 800 designs for Target, ranging from toilet brushes to Martini shakers, waste bins to wine coolers. The Graves-Target partnership is now seen as a model of a successful designer-retailer partnership.

Philippe Starck

Philippe Starck has rightly earned his 'superstar' status. A household name to many, he is responsible for some of the most familiar products, chairs, and interiors to have been designed since the 1980s.

Born 1949, Paris, France
Importance
Considered the 'superstar of design' for his prolific output across a diverse range of design fields, including products, furniture and interiors

Starck studied at the Ecole Nissim de Camondo before, in 1969, being appointed creative director of the Pierre Cardin studio, where he produced over 60 furniture designs. He then branched out as an independent designer, creating nightclub interiors for clients such as La Main Bleue, Montreuil (1976) and Les Bains Douches, Paris (1978). His career enjoyed a significant boost in 1982, when the then French President, François Mitterand, commissioned him to design the private chambers in the Elysée Palace.

A self-described autodidact, Starck founded his first company for inflatable furniture at the age of 19. Since then he has gone on to design scores of the most recognisable pieces of design produced towards the end of the twentieth century. To many younger designers, Starck is considered a godfather of design.

A quick visit to his website reveals a prodigious amount of design output during an amazing career. He is responsible for some of the most extraordinary interiors and architecture in the 1980s and 1990s, the creation of truly unique furniture and industrial design and

'…it's perhaps that American influence which has shaped my work, to the extent that I work instinctively, and above all fast. I can design a good piece of furniture in 15 minutes…'

other creative projects extending to foodstuffs, clothes, luggage, vehicles and bathrooms. Arguably his best-known product is the Juicy Salif lemon squeezer (1990 to 1991), which became a must-have cult object and design icon of the late twentieth century. Here, Starck produced his own unique interpretaion of the conventional lemon squeezer, giving it long, anthropomorphic legs and an elongated head. Like much of his work from this era, it is striking in its simplicity.

Starck's products can be seen in the permanent collections of a number of European and American museums, among them the Museum of Modern Art (MoMA) in New York and the Design Museum in London. Exhibitions of his work have been held in Paris, Rome, Munich, Tokyo, London and New York. He is also renowned for his eclectic interiors for Ian Schrager Hotels, Alain Mikli eyewear, Jean-Paul Gaultier and Hugo Boss.

In contrast to what Starck, himself, has described as narcissistic 'over-design' (his work of the 1980s and 1990s), he has, since the year 2000, focused his attention on producing designed objects and spaces that are honest and have integrity. He is now keen to advocate that designers should create products that have longevity and durability, steering themselves away from the throwaway culture of the recent past.

Jasper Morrison

Jasper Morrison is considered one of the world's most influential contemporary industrial designers. Known for designs that are at once austere and elegant, he has designed many products from kitchenware to a tram system, and for a host of prestigious clients, including Alessi, Cappellini, Flos, Magis and Sony.

Born 1959, London, England
Importance
Contemporary industrial designer, noted for sleek designs of everyday objects

Morrison was born in London in 1959. He studied design at Kingston Polytechnic, graduating in 1982, and received his master's degree in design from the Royal College of Art (RCA) in London in 1985. In 1984, he received a scholarship to study in Germany at the Berlin Academy of Arts. In 1986, a year after graduating from the RCA, his opened his Office for Design in London.

The Side Table and Slatted Stool, produced by SCP, were his first designs to be manufactured, and were launched at Milan in 1986. They were followed by the metal Thinking Man's Chair for Capellini (1987), designed for indoor and outdoor use, and the Ply-Chair for Vitra (1989), both of which exemplify his modernist vocabulary and his inventive use of form and materials.

With an approach to design that appears relatively straightforward on first inspection, and which results in creations that are restrained, clean and simple, Morrison has developed a rare knack among designers of being able to shape a diverse set of products, while at the same time retaining his successful and highly personal formal language. He is surprisingly a rather modest designer, whose intention is to bring innovation to everyday objects; he is committed to developing improvements in products. Although he skilfully crafts objects himself, most notably furniture and products, he does not claim to be a craftsman, however. All of his designs are destined for mass production.

Morrison has cultivated a well-established international reputation as a designer. Ever since his early success with door furniture for a German door handle manufacturer, which won many industry design awards, he has attracted some of the biggest names in the design world. He has created a

wide range of kitchenware for Alessi, including Pots and Pans cookware and the Family ranges of stainless steel trays and containers. For Magis he designed a number of moulded polypropylene items for the kitchen, including the ABD cutlery tray and Bottle stacking wine rack.

Towards the end of the twentieth century, he was commissioned to design the new Hanover tram *TW 2000,* which was unveiled to the public in 1997 and became the first vehicle to be awarded the IF Transportation Design Prize and the Ecology Award. More recently, Morrison and the critically renowned Japanese designer, Naoto Fukasawa, have collaborated together on the 'Supernormal' project and exhibition, which aims to provide consumers with a new, simpler, 'cleaner' attitude towards designed products.

Solo exhibitions and collaborations on several international exhibitions underline Morrison's status as a leading international designer. His designs are in the permanent collections of several museums throughout the world, including the Museum of Modern Art (MoMA), New York, and the Victoria and Albert Museum, London. One of the most recent of his many solo exhibitions was at the Axis Gallery, Tokyo, in 1999. Morrison teaches at the Royal College of Art in London and was elected as a Royal Designer for Industry, London in 2001.

Fordism

Henry Ford

Having tinkered with machines from a young age, Henry Ford's primary goal was to produce a motor car for the masses that would be within the financial reach of the ordinary man. Funded by a group of 12 investors the Ford Motor Company was established in June 1903, with the first car being produced and sold a month later. Over the course of the next five years, Ford directed a research and development schedule that resulted in a number of models, including the innovative and successful Model N, the disappointing Model K and the infamous Ford Model T.

Born Born: 1863, Greenfield Township, Michigan, United States
Importance Founder of Ford Motor Company and pioneer of mass production
Died 1947, Fair Lane, Michigan, United States

Primarily an engineer's design and not a stylist's car, the low-cost and reliable Model T – described by Ford as the 'universal car' – became an instant success. Its strengths lay in its relative cheapness, its durability and its ease of maintenance. It was in such demand that Ford introduced the modern concept of production-line manufacture, where assembling one product consisted of a host of employees working in unison fitting the same part, or parts, to each motor car via a moving assembly line. The approach, which later became known as 'Fordism', dramatically reduced assembly time and resulted in over 15 million Model Ts being produced between 1908 and 1927.

Ford quickly became a major employer and, although he adopted the trend of scientific management, where he aimed to make every man a unit in the overall machine, he soon encountered problems with high labour turnover. He introduced a generous five-dollars-a-day pay rate, in effect doubling his workers' wages, and cut the workday from nine to eight hours. Ford did this to ensure quality

work and allow a three-shift workday, which
resulted in the company being able to make
Model T motor cars 24 hours a day.

Highly productive and
consequently highly successful,
the Ford Motor Company
nevertheless came under
increasing pressure from
competitors such as
General Motors. By the
end of the 1920s, General
Motors recognised that a variety

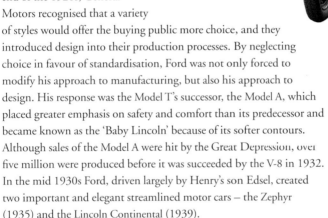

of styles would offer the buying public more choice, and they
introduced design into their production processes. By neglecting
choice in favour of standardisation, Ford was not only forced to
modify his approach to manufacturing, but also his approach to
design. His response was the Model T's successor, the Model A, which
placed greater emphasis on safety and comfort than its predecessor and
became known as the 'Baby Lincoln' because of its softer contours.
Although sales of the Model A were hit by the Great Depression, over
five million were produced before it was succeeded by the V-8 in 1932.
In the mid 1930s Ford, driven largely by Henry's son Edsel, created
two important and elegant streamlined motor cars – the Zephyr
(1935) and the Lincoln Continental (1939).

The motor car has altered most modern society for ever, changing
where and how we live. As more of us have owned cars, the
organisation of cities has changed. Most modern countries have
witnessed a substantial growth of their suburbs and the creation of
several national motorway systems, where car owners now have the
possibility of going just about anywhere at anytime.

MASS PRODUCTION

The term 'mass production' defines the activity of producing goods in large quantities, usually carried out using machinery or robots. The aims of mass production are threefold: companies wish to manufacture goods at a minimal unit cost; they need to produce goods where a predetermined level of quality can be guaranteed and maintained; and they want to be able to sustain high volume output often over a prolonged period of time. Mass production relies on the division and specialisation of labour, where workers are employed to carry out a range of specific tasks, often in carefully planned sequences and routines.

The Industrial Revolution, which began in Britain during the late eighteenth century, heralded the emergence of mass-production techniques, when the making of goods was revolutionised by new manufacturing processes and the division of labour. Up until that point, products had been conceived and manufactured by craftspeople and were often the work of highly skilled individuals working within a well-established aesthetic tradition. Around this time, manufacturers identified the competitive advantages of divorcing designing from making, so launching a new profession – the designer. Josiah Wedgwood was an early proponent of mass production, introducing the concept of a 'production line' to the making of ceramics in his factories in Stoke-on-Trent in the 1780s.

Generally speaking, mass production is attributed to the British textile industry and the American car-manufacturing industry. In Britain, the invention of machines effectively decreased the number of spinners required in the production process, which radically transformed the textile industry towards the early half of the nineteenth century. Previously, ornamentation was the property of the well-heeled, but mass production and technological advancements afforded this opportunity to the working classes in the form of cheap, machine-made products.

By the end of the nineteenth century, the United States had surpassed the United Kingdome and Europe as the world's leading manufacturing power. Many factors fuelled this progression. Chief among them was the shortage of labour in the United Kingdom and Europe, which made mass production on a large scale impossible. Standardisation was a notable feature of the American system. This involved the manufacture of many uniform components, so speeding up production further.

Henry Ford, the American car pioneer, first implemented mass-production in 1908, for the manufacture of his Model T car. Initially it took over 14 hours to assemble one single car, but, by using mass-production techniques, this time was dramatically reduced to just over one and a half hours. This massive saving enabled Ford to reduce the purchase cost of the vehicle from $1,000 in 1908 to just $360 in 1916. It was not long before companies across the globe adopted and refined Ford's methods.

Today, after several decades of major developments in computer-aided design and manufacture (see page 124), much development of new products is typically carried out via high-volume mass-production means. However, with emerging technological advances in 'rapid prototyping' and 'digital manufacture', products can now also be produced in smaller quantities or even as one-off products, while retaining all the benefits of mass production.

Ferdinand Porsche

There have been three Ferdinand Porsches, and each of them has had a significant impact on car design over the last couple of centuries. It was the collaboration between the first two Porsches, Professor Dr Ferdinand and Ferry, however, that remains the most significant, and that resulted in two major milestones in the history of car design: the *Auto-Union P-Wagen* and the revolutionary 'car for the masses' *Volkswagen* (People's Car). Ferry Porsche's son, also Ferdinand, produced the iconic Porsche *911* model over 40 years ago.

Born 1875, Maffersdorf, Austria-Hungary
Importance Innovative car engineer and designer, collaborating with his son to produce the world's most-produced car
Died 1951, Stuttgart, Germany

Professor Dr Ferdinand Porsche (1875–1951) was a brilliant, innovative engineer who worked for Daimler-Benz before setting up his own automotive design company in 1931. His son, Ferdinand 'Ferry' Porsche (born 1909), took over the reins of the Porsche car company after the Second World War, and skilfully established the firm as a market leader in the design and development of high-performance cars. Widely considered to be decades ahead of its time, their *Auto-Union* marked a radical departure from other racing-car designs of the period. The creation of the *Volkswagen*, however, in 1935, was one of the most significant moments in car-design history.

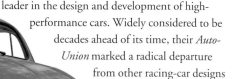

It is reported that Adolf Hitler produced the brief for the Volkswagen during the Berlin Automobile Show in 1934. With a demanding development time of 10 months for the production of the first Volkswagen, Porsche set about designing innovations in the engine, chassis and transmission. The first prototype was unveiled in October 1935, with later versions of the car seeing improvements with the addition of bumpers and running boards. The distinctive and streamlined body of the car was designed by the acclaimed aerodynamicist, Erwin Komenda, and, in 1938, it was immediately nicknamed the 'Beetle' by the *New York Times* upon being unveiled to the press. Serial production of the Volkswagen had to wait until 1941, when the ruling National Socialist Party initiated the manufacture of 41 cars, predominately for propaganda purposes. By 1950, however, over 100,000 Volkswagen cars had been made and, in 1962, Volkswagen were producing one million cars every year. A decade later the Beetle became the world's most-produced car.

In 1948, after the end of the Second World War, Ferry used a number of Volkswagen parts and a flat four-cylinder engine to produce the Porsche 356 roadster – the first car to carry the Porsche badge. Komenda was now tasked with making the 356 beautiful and functionally efficient. By 1958, over 10,000 of the roadsters had been produced.

Komenda and Ferry Porsche's son, Ferdinand Alexander Porsche (born 1935), began work on a new car, in 1961, that had a rear-mounted, air-cooled, six-cylinder engine, and which would eventually lead to the classic 911, one of the most celebrated sports cars in history. Today, Porsche continues to be recognised as one of the leading automotive brands in the world and has an enviable reputation for its commitment to design, engineering and technological excellence.

Corradino d'Ascanio

Although Corradino d'Ascanio primarily designed helicopters, his name has long been synonymous with the most iconic scooter of all time – the Vespa – 16 million of which have been made, in 130 different models, since its beginning in 1947.

Born 1891, Popoli, Italy
Importance Italian post-war designer of the iconic Vespa scooter
Died 1981, Pisa, Italy

D'Ascanio studied engineering at the Regio Istituto Superiore di Ingegneria (which later became Turin Polytechnic) and obtained his degree as an industrial engineer in 1914. In 1925 he founded a company with Baron Pietro Trojani and worked with him on some early helicopter designs. In 1930, he designed a prototype helicopter, the D'AT3 for the Ministero dell'Aeronautica, which won the world record for flying distance in a straight line, for altitude and flight duration. D'Ascanio joined the Piaggio engineering company in 1934, for whom he designed a range of aircraft components.

During and after the Second World War, d'Ascanio continued to work on helicopter design, but he is best known for the design of the Vespa motor scooter, in 1947. Shown for the first time at the bicycle and motorcycle show in Milan, in 1949, the Vespa became the most popular scooter in the world for the next 50 years.

The Vespa was born in the post-war period in Italy, and was the brainchild of Enrico Piaggio. The Second World War virtually destroyed all of Piaggio's plants, but the company decided to rebuild their factories and address the pressing need for an inexpensive means of transportation. Initially designed to appeal to women as a cheap means of transport over short distances, the scooter soon became very popular with men as well. Thus, at exactly noon on the 23 April 1946, in Florence's Ministry of Industry and Commerce, Enrico Piaggio filed a patent for a 'motorcycle of a rational complexity of organs and elements combined with a frame with mudguards and a casing covering the whole mechanical part'.

Initially, the first prototype was christened Paperino (meaning Donald Duck in Italian) by engineers in the factory, owing to its striking visual similarities with the cartoon character. Upon viewing the Vespa prototype for the first time, which he loathed, Piaggio demanded that d'Ascanio be given overall control of the redesign. It is widely reported that Piaggio heard the buzzing sound of d'Ascanio's new engine design for the Vespa and proclaimed 'sembra una vespa', which translates roughly as 'sounds like a wasp'. Consequently, the name Vespa has remained for over 60 years and in that time has become an international design icon enjoying both commercial and critical acclaim.

Piaggio formed a widespread service association all over Europe and the rest of the world and, by 1953, there were over 10,000 Piaggio service points across the globe. Vespa motorcycle clubs sprung up all over the world and, in 1951, approximately 20,000 Vespa aficionados showed up at the 'Italian Vespa Day'. In 1953 there were more then 50,000 Vespa drivers organised in clubs throughout the world. By 1956, one million Vespas had been produced and the scooter became synonymous with freedom and mobility. It helped shape a new international expression of a cultivated and cosmopolitan lifestyle throughout Europe and the United States.

Automotive

Pinin Farina

Battista 'Pinin' Farina was responsible for the creation of some of the most beautiful cars in the world. Legendary vehicles such as the outstanding Cisitalia (1947), the exquisite Ferrari Dino Berlinetta (1965), and the classic Ferrari Testarossa (1984) were all shaped from within the headquarters of this great design styling house.

Born 1893, Turin, Italy
Importance Designer of iconic post-war sportscars for companies including Ferrari and Alfa Romeo
Died 1966, Lausanne, Switzerland

The origins of this famous *carrozzeria* (meaning 'auto body') styling company began when Battista Farina began working at his brother, Giovanni's, bodyshop in 1904. He was just 11 years old.

By 1930, Farina had established his own auto body workshop – the Carrozzeria Pinin Farina. His overarching aim, like Ford before him, was to make special car bodies, not by manual craftsmanship techniques alone, but by introducing large-scale manufacturing processes and production into the industry. One of his key objectives was to provide employment to increasing numbers of local workers. To this end, he created a factory with new tools and procedures so that he was able to turn out small batch runs of vehicles at a rate of seven to eight cars every day.

The 1930s and 1940s, in particular, were a golden era for Pinin Farina. During these years, the firm developed a number of innovative car designs including the Alfa Romeo 6C (1931) and the aerodynamic Lancia Aprilla Coupé (1936 to 1937). The groundbreaking Cisitalia of 1947 was selected as the first of eight outstanding cars of our time for permanent display at the Museum of Modern Art (MoMA) in New York, owing to its beautiful and simple visual lines, which set new standards for car designers in the post-war period. By the early 1950s, Pinin Farina had started to collaborate with car manufacturers

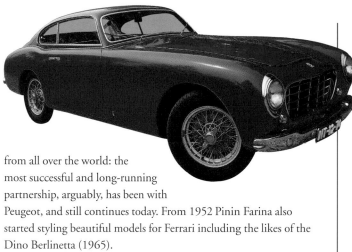

from all over the world: the
most successful and long-running
partnership, arguably, has been with
Peugeot, and still continues today. From 1952 Pinin Farina also
started styling beautiful models for Ferrari including the likes of the
Dino Berlinetta (1965).

By the late 1950s, the Carrozzeria Pinin Farina plant moved to
larger premises and officially changed its name to Pininfarina. In 1966
Pininfarina created its own Studies and Research Centre, which helped
develop many notable concept and production cars, such as the Ferrari
Modulo (1970), the Ferrari P6 (1968), and the Jaguar XJS (1978).
Pinifarina established itself as the world leader in bodywork design by
the mid-1970s, helped significantly by the construction of their own
full-size wind tunnel in 1972 (one of a few in the world at that time).

By the mid-1980s, Pininfarina had invested in a new plant, new
processes and product technologies. From 1981 the company also
began assembling major components and building complete vehicles
at the rate of about 40,000 car bodies every year.

Today, Pininfarina continues to research into new ways of design,
aerodynamics, materials and processes, safety and lessening the impact
on the environment in its vehicle production. The company has
managed to maintain an edge in the demanding world of car design
and manufacture and continues to make an enormous contribution to
the development of new automotive engineering and design products.

Flaminio Bertoni

Flaminio Bertoni is widely regarded as one of the twentieth century's most talented automotive designers, directly involved in the design of such classic, and highly innovative, mass-market cars as the elegant Citroën Traction Avant, the original 2CV (the *Deux Chevaux*), and the iconic DS 19.

Born 1903, Masnago, Italy
Importance Italian designer of some of the most influential cars of the twentieth century
Died 1964, Paris, France

Bertoni's early career was spent working for a local coachbuilder, Macchi, in northern Italy. In 1931 he left Italy and moved to Paris, where he hoped to establish his own design studio, but instead he took up a job offer from Citroën.

In 1934 Citroën launched the revolutionary Traction Avant with its front-wheel drive and long wheelbase. Generally considered to be at least two decades ahead of its time from an engineering point of view, the Traction Avant was also pioneering from a marketing perspective. Buyers were able to select from a choice of three base models in 21 different versions and three colours. The vehicle achieved commercial success and is now regarded as one of the most important pre-Second World War cars.

In 1935 Bertoni started working on the Citroën TPV (*Toute Petit Vehicule* - meaning 'very small car'), which later became the 2CV. Based on Pierre Boulanger's original concept, the highly original and idiosyncratic shape of the 2CV was down to the styling of Bertoni. Boulanger, managing director of Citroën at the time, came up with the idea of the 2CV when he was driving in the countryside of the Auvergne region in France and got stuck in a traffic jam of horse-drawn carriages and handcarts. He later deduced that rural farmers didn't own cars because they were too expensive, too much of a responsibility, too big and heavy for a woman to drive and they were totally impractical for carrying milk to market or herding cattle.

Boulanger believed that if he could produce a cheap, simple and rugged car, a vast untapped market would open up. So Citroën's design office took on the project, and Boulanger challenged his designers and engineers with the now legendary design brief: 'I want a car that will carry two farmers in their working clothes and 50kg (110lb) of potatoes or a small barrel of wine, have a maximum speed of 60kmph (38mph) and

do over 32km per litre (90 miles per gallon). The car must also be capable of carrying a basket of eggs over a ploughed field without breaking a single one, and its price must be less than a third of that of the Traction Avant.' Launched in 1948, the 2CV became Citroën's best-selling car ever at an estimated four million units sold between 1948 and 1990.

In 1957 Citroën launched the DS 19 designed by Bertoni, a revolutionary car, both technically and stylistically, that was marketed as a piece of sculpture on wheels. With its innovative use of materials and almost surreal streamlining the vehicle quickly became known as the 'Goddess' in France. Like the Traction Avant that went before it, the DS 19 was considered to be an extremely advanced vehicle for its time with its independent self-levelling hydro-pneumatic suspension, hydraulically powered steering, disc brakes and automatic clutch.

Launched over fifty years ago to massive critical and commercial acclaim, Bertoni's design is now widely considered to be the car of the twentieth century.

Alec Issigonis

Alec Issigonis is widely considered to be one of the major figures in twentieth-century automotive design. The Morris Mini Minor was not the first car that he designed, but it did win him worldwide recognition, with over five million units selling by the time of his death.

Born 1906, Smryna, Ottoman Empire (now Izmir, Turkey)
Importance Greek-born designer of iconic Mini
Died 1988, Birmingham, England

Critics have described Issigonis as a determined, strong-willed and stubbornly uncompromising engineer. Early in his career he worked as a draughtsman for an engineering company who were producing a new type of semi-automatic transmission, before taking up a position at Morris Motors as steering and suspension engineer in 1936. The Morris Motor Company had been formed in 1912, in Oxford, and Issigonis shared the company's commitment to high volume, low-cost automobile production.

This common philosophy manifested itself in the design of the Morris Minor, which was launched in 1946. Influenced by American automotive styling from the 1930s and 1940s, this was a revolutionary design of its day, selling over 15,000 cars a year in the United States. It was truly the first modern British car; by 1960 more than one million had been sold, and it remained in production for over 20 years. To this day, the Morris Minor still has a devoted following of collectors and enthusiasts.

In response to the Suez oil crisis of 1956, the world's car manufacturers had to produce cars that were more fuel-efficient, and Issigonis designed the Morris Mini Minor specifically to be economical to run. Born in 1959, it quickly became the most commercially successful car ever produced across Europe. It rapidly gained iconic status, becoming a symbol of the optimism that permeated early 1960s culture.

The enormous critical and commercial success of the car lay not just in its significant engineering improvements, but also in its truly novel design. The box-like vehicle was only 3m (12 ft) long, but it could achieve 17 km per litre (50 miles per gallon) and speeds of up to 112 kmph (70 mph); it could accommodate four adult passengers relatively easily and was very easy to park and manoeuvre. Issigonis maximised the interior space of the Mini by placing the engine sideways – a unique concept of the day, which exemplified the designer's practical and common sense approach to design.

The Mini was also hugely influential culturally. Deemed by many cultural commentators to be the first truly 'classless' car, Mini drivers included major celebrities of the time as well as ordinary citizens, with the Beatles and actors Steve McQueen, Peter Sellers and Dudley Moore among them. Arguably, the car's most famous media moment, however, was its role as an escape car in the 1969 film, *The Italian Job*, starring Michael Caine. The Mini had a major influential impact on many later compact cars, such as the Renault 5 and the Volkswagen Golf.

Although most commonly thought of as the designer of the Mini, Issigonis also created two of the other five best-selling cars in UK automobile design history – the Morris Minor and the Austin 1100 – and had that rare combination of practical engineering ability and the vision of a designer. Before his death in 1988, Issigonis was knighted for his immense contribution to the British car industry and made a fellow of the Royal Society.

Giorgetto Giugiaro

Giorgetto Giugiaro has had an enormous influence on car design throughout the world, designing vehicles for most of the major European and Japanese manufacturers, including Audi, BMW, Volkswagen, Fiat, Alfa Romeo, Lotus, Lancia and Maserati. With a professional career spanning more than 50 years, he has designed more than 200 cars in total. It was Giugiaro who initiated the 'folded paper' concept – designing cars with straight lines and sharp edges – that dominated the 1970s.

Born 1938, Garessio, Italy
Importance Cult figure in automotive design history

Although arguably best known for his stylish and sleek sportscars, such as the Alfa Romeo Alfasud (1971) and the Maserati 3200 GT Coupé (1998), Giugiaro also designed some of the most popular utilitarian vehicles ever created, including the Volkswagen Golf (1974), the Fiat Panda (1980) and the Fiat Uno (1983).

After studying technical drawing and graphic design at the Academy of Fine Art in Turin, Giugiaro worked in Fiat's design department. In 1959 he became head of the styling department at the sportscar manufacturer Bertone, in Turin, where he worked with Nuccio Bertone designing several cars, including the BMW 3200 CS (1961) and the Alfa Romeo Giulia GT (1963).

Giugiaro left Bertone in 1965 to become the head of design for another Turin manufacturer, Ghia where he designed the Fiat Dino Coupé (1967). Then, in 1968, Giugiaro, Aldo Mantovani and Luciano Bosio formed the car-styling consultancy, ItalDesign, and it was here that the Fiat Panda and the Volkswagens Golf, Scirocco and Passat were conceived. Today, the company employs around 750 people and offers design services such as pre-production studies and the construction of working prototypes.

Giugiaro has also worked on a range of products through his independent product design company, Giugiaro Design, formed in 1981. Among the products developed here are the Logica sewing machine for Necchi (1982), ItalDesign Aztec concept car (1987), the Nikon F4 and F5 cameras (1988 and 1996), a high-speed ferry catamaran for SEC (1992), the Macchina Sportiva watch for Seiko (1996) and Grand Prix ski boots for Nordica (1997).

During his prolific career, Giugiaro, has received a number of awards, the most prestigious of which include the SIAD Silver Medal of the British Society of Artists and Industrial Designers in 1980, the Compasso d'Oro for the Fiat Panda in 1980, and the Compasso d'Oro for coachwork design in 1984. In the same year, the Royal College of Art in London awarded him an honorary degree in design. In 1999, a jury of more than 120 automotive experts from more than 30 countries voted him Car Designer of the Century. He occupies a Place of Honour at the Detroit Automotive Hall of Fame and he received the honorary title of Cavaliere del Lavoro (Knight of Labour) from the President of the Republic of Italy, Carlo Azeglio Ciampi.

Regularly mentioned as a major influence on many of the new generation of automobile designers, Giugiaro is also widely considered a strong, multidisciplinary designer. Much of his current work revolves around providing design and innovation services in the fields of transportation design and architecture.

Automotive

CAD/CAM

The history of computer-aided design and manufacturing (CAD/CAM) stretches almost as far back as the development of the computer itself. In the early days of computer usage, the concept was relatively primitive, prohibitively expensive and was rarely used outside of the military, aerospace and automotive industries.

That all changed, however, in the early 1960s, with the development of a revolutionary program written by Ivan Sutherland as part of his PhD studies at the renowned Massachusetts Institute of Technology (MIT). Generally considered to be the first computer-aided design (CAD) program with industrial use, Sutherland's Sketchpad used an x–y point plotter display that allowed users to draw directly onto a screen using a light pen. It was completely groundbreaking, and contributed massively to the way in which people and computers have interacted ever since. For many today, it remains the first truly modern CAD program.

As computer hardware became increasingly powerful – in terms of both memory and processing speed – CAD became less expensive and more widely accessible to all manner of designers, who readily embraced the concept. During the 1960s, the programs were used mainly in the design and manufacture of car exteriors. By the mid-1970s, however, the use of CAD/CAM had spread to many other industry sectors and by the end of the decade, software developers had created tools that allowed users to draw and manipulate basic geometric shapes (boxes, cones, and so on) and join them together via Boolean operations. The software developer, Autodesk, produced the first version of AutoCAD in 1982, which would go on to establish itself as the undisputed market leader for several major automotive and aerospace industries.

During the 1980s and 1990s CAD/CAM development gathered apace with several high-level collaborations between software companies and major industry partners such as General Motors, UNIX, General Electric and Boeing. One such development was the launch of hybrid modelling, which allowed designers to combine all the functionality of traditional CAD modelling with advanced parametric technologies. By the mid-1990s, over one million AutoCAD products had been sold and there were nearly 500,000 users of CAD/CAM across the globe.

By the end of the twentieth century, CAD had become a hugely powerful tool used by designers for preparing drawings and translating them into three-dimensional models that can be rotated, scaled, skewed, extruded and cross-sectioned. CAD data can then be translated by computer-aided manufacturing (CAM) software, which turns the data into manufactured objects such as models, parts, components and products.

Today, CAD/CAM manufacturers predominately focus on trying to make their software more efficient and user-friendly. Very recent advances in CAD/CAM, information visualisation, rapid prototyping, materials and injection moulding have given designers the opportunity to use new shapes and to explore transparency and translucency, which has given rise to a new breed of object – the blobject (see pages 38–39). The period objects of our time, blobjects are the physical products that the digital revolution has brought to the consumer shelf that were impossible until the early 1990s, advanced by designers such as Marc Newson, Philippe Starck and Ross Lovegrove.

J Mays

J Mays is internationally acknowledged as one of the most important figures in the history of automobile design. He is widely credited with developing a unique approach to the design process, through which branding and identity are fundamental factors in the design and creation of an automobile.

Born 1954, Pauls Valley, Oklahoma, United States
Importance
Revolutionised the car design industry by integrating branding and marketing into design

Like many car designers of his generation, Mays graduated from Pasadena's Art Center College of Design in 1980 with a degree in transportation design. His final degree project was an ambitious aerodynamic car that he had managed to develop and test in a local company's wind tunnel. The project alerted many of the leading automobile manufacturers in America and across Europe and, after nine offers of employment, Mays accepted a position with Audi AG based in Ingolstadt, Germany.

While at Audi AG, Mays designed the Avus Quattro concept car, which caused a massive stir at the Tokyo Motor Show of 1991, with its aluminium body and gull-wing doors. The car proved to be highly significant for both Mays and Audi, serving as a forerunner for the design of the Audi TT,

SY51 YOX

launched at the Frankfurt International Motor Show in 1995. Designed by Mays' colleague, Freeman Thomas, the Audi TT received widespread critical acclaim.

In 1990, Volkswagen-Audi sent Mays back to southern California to define 'Californian trends' and incorporate them into the design of a new Volkswagen automobile. Mays turned his attention the VW Beetle with the conviction that this was the only Volkswagen to have made an impact in the US. Working closely with Freeman Thomas, Mays set out to develop design ideas for Concept One, the car that would eventually become the New Beetle. First shown at the 1994 North American International Auto Show in Detroit, Concept One received such a positive response from the press and public alike that Volkswagen-Audi decided to put the car into production.

'No one has cultivated the connection between cars and our deepest emotions as explicitly as J Mays'.

Vanity Fair

In 1997, Mays was recruited by the Ford Motor Company to become its Vice President of Global Design. The post means that he is not only responsible for the design of every vehicle with a blue oval Ford badge, but for all the vehicles in the enormous range of brands that Ford has acquired over the years. Since joining Ford, Mays has established the Living Legends Studio at Ford's Dearborn, Michigan, headquarters. Here, his team of designers and engineers has developed a number of cars based on iconic cars from Ford's past, including the new Thunderbird (2002), the new concept for the Ford Forty-Nine (based on the 1949 Ford), the redesigned 'Bullitt' special-edition Mustang (2002), and the GT40 concept car (2002).

Mays' unique approach, described as 'retrofuturistic', is exemplified in several of his concept cars. While he has received criticism in the automotive press for many of his designs, his work has been of great benefit to the automotive industry, introducing ideas from other fields and questioning the future role of automotive design.

Index

For main entries see contents page. References to designers are given only where mentioned other than their main entry.